Keep Smiling!

A practical guide
to lifelong
dental health

by

Catherine Thom

DipDentHyg BA MA

Illustrations by Margaret Mountney

To The Armour Family
Here's to better dental
health.

Catherine

Published by MET Publishing Canada
Ottawa, Canada 2010

http://www.metpublishing.ca

Produced by Wallbridge House Publishing
246 Albert Street, Belleville, Ontario, K8N 3N9

Cover and book design by Allan Graphics Ltd.
Printed in Canada by Allan Graphics Ltd.
170 Binnington Court, Kingston, Ontario, K7M 8N1

Cover photos by Don Douglas of My One Thousand Photography
Ottawa: don@my1k.ca   www.my1k.ca

Library and Archives Canada Cataloguing in Publication

Thom, C.
Keep smiling! : a practical guide to lifelong dental health / Catherine
Thom ; illustrations by Margaret Mountney.

Includes bibliographical references and index.
ISBN 978-0-9867231-0-0

1. Teeth--Care and hygiene. I. Title.

RK61.T56 2010   617.6'01
C2010-906487-9

This book distils a lifetime's experience, expertly analyzed and organized to give the general public a comprehensive and understandable guide to all aspects of oral health. In my opinion it should be in every lending library in Canada and better yet, in every home.

- BARBARA M. FRASER, RETIRED COLLEGE LIBRARIAN

Recommended for anyone with teeth! This book should be in every dental office waiting room in the country as a reference book for patients.

- J.E. McMECHAN, ECONOMIST

Dedication

This book is dedicated to absent family members
(parents Eva and Gordon Thom and sister
Gwennyth Poulton) and to all those with whom we
come in contact on life's journey. Those relationships,
fleeting or enduring, help make us who we are.

About the Author

Catherine Thom has been associated with oral health care since graduating with a Diploma in Dental Hygiene from the University of Toronto, Ontario, Canada. Her work experience included private practice (orthodontic and general) and dental public health prior to becoming an educator after completing an undergraduate arts degree at Carleton University, Ottawa.

Ms. Thom spent 28 years at Algonquin College of Applied Arts and Technology in Ottawa as a professor and program co-ordinator. After serving in acting administrative capacities as Dental Programs Director and Chair of the Allied Health Department she chose to return to the classroom. Ms. Thom co-ordinated curriculum, clinical and field placement activities for the full-time, continuing education and post-graduate programs. She also participated in the Ontario Ministry of Colleges and Universities curriculum development workshops to establish the baseline competencies to be taught in Ontario dental hygiene and dental assistant programs. While on sabbatical leave she completed a master's degree in psychology at Carleton University which led to research and co-ordination of standardized testing procedures for admission to dental hygiene programs used across Ontario for over a decade.

Ms. Thom served for four years as a professional member on the Board of the College of Dental Hygienists of Ontario. She participated on the Education, Communication and Discipline Committees. As a member of the Quality Assurance Committee she assisted in developing professional assessment materials. She also chaired the Clinical Assessment Restructuring Committee.

Since leaving Algonquin College, Ms. Thom has provided educational consulting services to dental hygiene programs and conducted continuing education workshops. This book represents the culmination of over four decades of experience in imparting health care information to dental professionals and clients.

Acknowledgements

No project of this type happens without input and support from a variety of people. In this case, I would like to thank former colleagues Barbara Fraser and Renie Grosser for reading the early versions and suggesting they had merit.

My sisters, Margaret Mountney and Marian Ellis, provided valuable practical help and emotional support. Margaret produced the illustrations and Marian made sure I had dotted the "i"s and crossed the "t"s.

Current staff at Algonquin College, Ottawa, provided equipment and materials on loan.

Long-time friends Sylvia and Orland French at Wallbridge House Publishing ably converted the final draft and illustrations into a coherent whole.

Happy members of St. Stephen's Presbyterian Church, Ottawa, allowed their smiles to grace the cover.

Without the help and encouragement of these people and others, I would not have continued.

– *Catherine Thom*

Keep Smiling!
A Practical Guide to Lifelong Dental Health

The B-S-T of tooth decay
Severe tooth decay in infants (infant caries syndrome)
Periodontal disease
Top 10 "plaque facts"
Self checks for oral cancer

Part V   An Ounce of Prevention

Diabetes mellitus
Radiation therapy of the head and neck
Chemotherapy for cancer
HIV and AIDS
Reduced immune system function

Part VI   *A Pound of Cure*

Part VII   *Dental Emergencies and Other Stuff*

List of Tables

List of Illustrations

Part I

Nothing Personal, Doc, But...

Chapter 1

The Problems with Dentistry

In This Chapter

▶ chief complaints about dental treatment: pain and fear
▶ origins of fear of dental treatment
▶ dental phobia – causes and treatment
▶ coping strategies for the non-phobic dental client
▶ options for pain and anxiety control
▶ preparing a child for professional dental care

Chief Complaints about Dental Treatment: Pain and Fear

If dentists and other dental care providers had a dollar for every time they heard the phrase "nothing personal, Doc, but … " followed by one of several common negative statements, they could all retire years earlier than they usually do. The problems with dentistry depend on from which end of the sharp instruments you are making the assessment.

For the recipients of care, the most common complaints are about pain, fear and (where insurance doesn't cover services) paying for the experience. Less commonly voiced concerns include: officious staff, assembly-line practices and waiting in the reception room. From the providers' point of view the main problems include dealing with anxious and/or angry clients and those who report for emergency services only.

Although sadistic dentists rank up there with greedy lawyers and crooked accountants as the butt of popular jokes, it is an interesting fact that polls show dentists among the most trusted of professionals. Research also indicates that the expressed negativity from clients takes a toll on dental care providers as well. Among the professions (medicine, law, accounting, engineering, etc.) dentists tend to have higher rates of substance abuse, family discord, depression and suicide. They also are murdered more frequently than practitioners in other disciplines.

With this information in mind, please try to handle your dental staff kindly. They may unavoidably be causing you some discomfort, but are often enduring considerable life stress associated with your care.

Origins of Fear of Dental Treatment

There are two major sources of fear of dental treatment. The first comes directly from Pavlov's classic conditioning model. If you experience a pairing of a neutral stimulus (dental office, dentist) with an unpleasant effect (pain of treatment) then fear of an unpleasant consequence is associated with subsequent presentation of the stimulus. In short, if you have had an unpleasant dental treatment experience in the past, you are likely to be somewhat uneasy at subsequent appointments.

The second source of fear comes from the negative reports of others. There are several common types of such reports. One is careless adult talk about medical and dental procedures that is overheard by young children. Adults often describe for one another quite graphically, and often exaggerated for effect, medical or dental procedures that they have undergone. They usually assume that if children overhear such information it isn't a problem because they do not understand what is being said. In fact that lack of understanding is precisely the problem. Children cannot realize that what they hear about adult medical concerns is not relevant to them. They do, however, remember parts of the information. When the time comes for them to enter into a medical or dental treatment situation, they recall parts of the stories they have overheard and already have some level of irrational fear.

Another source of negative influence can be older children. Siblings are the usual but not the only culprits of spreading or inventing medical/dental horror stories. During preadolescence, stories of superheroes, ghosts and goblins are common fare. Part of growing up involves coping with your place in the pecking order. Older children like to influence younger ones – not always positively. Children will be children. What better way to wield power over younger children than to tease them with a story you know isn't true but they will believe because you are a credible source in their eyes? Many parents are unaware of these influences until, in spite of careful preparation, the younger child's first dental visit goes less than smoothly, thanks to the influence of older children.

Although it is difficult to believe, there are still some parents who use threats of medical or dental treatment as a way to discipline their child. If the child misbehaves, the parent threatens to take him/her to the dentist if they do not co-operate. Anyone using this tactic should not be surprised later if the child's dental appointments become struggles for all concerned.

For most people, the level of psychological discomfort when facing medical or dental treatment is manageable, thus they continue to access regular professional services. If, however, a treatment experience has been sufficiently traumatic, it can cause true dental phobia resulting in avoidance of dental treatment for years or even decades. Sadly this avoidance leads to increased levels of dental disease requiring more extensive and possibly more uncomfortable treatment which in turn leads to increased fear and avoidance. The pain, fear, avoidance cycle can become well established.

Dental Phobia – Causes and Treatment

If you are dental phobic you're not alone! Studies estimate that in North America dental phobia affects five to 15 percent of the population. In Canada that translates into 1.6 to 4.9 million people who do not access regular dental care because of extreme fear of treatment. In other countries of the world where dental services are less prevalent, estimates of dental phobia approach 20 percent of those populations.

A number of polls taken in North America and reported in *Health* magazine have yielded a list of the most commonly reported fears. These are rank-ordered below.

The Top 10 Things We Fear

► speaking in public
► getting fat
► going out alone at night
► dental visits
► dying
► spiders and insects
► swimming in the ocean
► heights
► flying
► large crowds

Treatment of Dental Phobia

Although there is a variety of pharmacological pain and anxiety measures (described later in this chapter) which can be used in conjunction with dental treatment, none of these options treats the phobia itself. Mood altering medication should always be considered as a last resort for helping clients deal with routine dental procedures. All drugs have side effects ranging from mildly undesirable to dangerous. In addition, frequent use of any medication can lead to psychological and physical dependence. All good dental care involves aspects of client learning and participation, elements that are not available to the practitioner if the client is under the influence of anti-anxiety medication or profound anaesthesia.

If you see yourself in the definition of a dental phobic and are concerned that the state of your mouth is not contributing positively to your overall health, there is help available. If you are not experiencing any acute symptoms (pain and swelling), but you want to get back into the dental treatment loop you might want to consider visiting a good psychologist first. One commonly used treatment for phobic behaviour (not just regarding dental treatment) is called systematic desensitization. Most psychologists, and a few dental practitioners concerned with helping clients overcome serious distress caused by dental treatment, offer this technique in their practices.

Systematic desensitization (SD) uses a combination of relaxation therapy, conscious imaging and positive "self-talk" (encouraging statements that you repeat to yourself to help you adopt beneficial reactions to feared situations). SD is useful in helping people deal with irrational levels of fear associated with specific items (snakes, spiders) or events (flying, dental treatment). Fearful individuals are asked to imagine aspects around the feared item or event that upset them. Once the elements are identified and described in detail, they are ranked by the client from least to most fear-provoking. This set of statements is referred to as a *fear hierarchy*.

For many dental phobics, the thought of calling to make a dental appointment causes stress. As they get closer to the office site and actual treatment procedures, fear levels typically escalate. When this is the case, a fear hierarchy may closely resemble a description of appointment events in chronological order. A sample dental treatment fear hierarchy where this is apparent is detailed later in this chapter.

If you seek counseling for dental phobia and the counselor suggests treatment with SD you will generate your own feared events list. The counselor will then teach you one of several possible relaxation techniques and ask you to practise it until you are able to put yourself in a relaxed state easily and quickly. Now you are asked to induce your state of relaxation while the statement regarding the least fear producing element of your hierarchy is presented. You are asked to imagine yourself in the situation described. You will then be instructed to stop imagining the scene described and to imagine a very pleasant relaxing scene while the fear hierarchy item is presented a second time. This sequence of presentation-relaxation is repeated for each item in the hierarchy.

Your counselor might want you to practise SD only under his/her supervision. If s/he is certain that you have the process under control, you may be asked to practise regularly at home using a taped presentation of the fear hierarchy statements. The more frequent the practice sessions the more quickly your level of stress will diminish. For some people, imaginary practice of SD will alleviate sufficient anxiety that they can proceed with dental treatment as required. For others, following the steps of SD in the "real world" will be necessary.

If real world practice is suggested, you will be asked to place yourself physically for a designated period of time in the situation described by each hierarchy statement in turn. This usually means you will have to contact the office and make your own appointment (as opposed to having someone make it for you). You may also be encouraged to visit the office, talk to the receptionist, complete your paperwork and spend some time in the reception room taking in the sights, sounds and smells of the environment before you are actually scheduled for treatment. During your exposure to the feared elements you will continue to practise the prescribed relaxation technique. Obviously as you approach the final statements in the hierarchy you will actually be in the treatment situation.

Sample Dental Fear Hierarchy

1. You have a tooth that is bothering you. You decide you must make a dental appointment. You look up the dentist's number and dial the phone. When the receptionist answers, you say you are having problems with a tooth and request an appointment. You are offered a choice of dates and times. You select one and complete the call.

2. You are traveling to your dental appointment. You leave the familiar landmarks of your neighbourhood and enter an area of town that is not part of your daily routine. You begin thinking about your dental appointment and you feel slightly uneasy. You tell yourself you can handle whatever needs to be done.

3. You are now walking down the street to the front door of the building where your dentist's office is located. You enter the front door. You confirm the floor the office is on and ring for the elevator. You get off at the correct floor, walk down the hall and enter the dental office.

4. You enter the reception area a few minutes early. As you enter you notice the medicinal odours associated with the treatment area. You approach the receptionist who verifies your current address and asks you to update your confidential health history. She says the dentist is on schedule and invites you to take a seat until your appointment time.

5. You finish the paperwork as requested and hand the file back to the receptionist. As you watch the other clients in the reception area you begin thinking about the dentist working in your mouth and you begin to feel anxious. You wonder what treatment will be necessary. You breathe deeply and relax. You tell yourself you will be able to cope with the required treatment.

6. The dental assistant appears in the reception room and calls your name. She escorts you to a treatment room and asks you to be seated. You sit down and look around the room while the assistant places a napkin around your neck. You notice the unopened pack of sterile instruments and wonder what is inside.

7. The dentist enters the room and greets you. He asks about the reasons for your visit and you tell him you have a lower back tooth that is painful. He listens attentively and asks some questions to clarify your problem. He indicates he would like to examine your mouth. He washes his hands, dries them and puts on gloves and a mask.

8. He picks up a mirror and a probe and asks you to open your mouth. The dentist asks you to indicate which tooth is bothering you. You point to the tooth and the dentist gently probes the tooth. You feel the probe against the gum and hear it scratch the tooth surface.

9. The dentist says there is an area of decay around an old filling. He indicates that the old filling and the decayed area need to be removed and a new filling placed. You tell yourself you will not find the placement of a new filling difficult.

10. When the dentist says he would like to inject some local anaesthetic you tell him you are afraid of needles. He indicates that some gel will be applied to the injection site to numb the area before the injection. You tell yourself to relax knowing that will make it easier.

11. The topical anaesthetic gel is applied and takes effect but you still feel a bit anxious. You relax as much as possible. The injection is barely detectable and you are surprised when the dentist tells you it is finished. You tell yourself you were more worried than necessary.

12. You sit for a few minutes while the anaesthetic takes effect. You are aware of increasing numbness of your tongue and lip. The dentist returns to begin preparing the tooth. He advises you to raise your hand to have him stop work if you need a break. This element of control of the situation makes you feel better.

13. The dentist is removing the old filling material and preparing the tooth for the new restoration. You hear the drill and the suction device the assistant is using to take water away from the site. You are getting tired of holding your mouth open and begin to get tense and restless. You remind yourself to let go of the tension and relax. You begin to think of your relaxation place.

14. The tooth preparation is finished. The dentist packs the filling material into the tooth and takes several minutes to carve the restoration. He and the assistant pass several different instruments back and forth. You begin to feel bored. You start thinking about your plans for the weekend.

15. The dentist asks you to bite your teeth together gently. You do so. He asks you to

open your mouth again as the filling needs some minor adjustment. The bite is checked again and the dentist says you are finished. You thank him and prepare to leave the treatment room. You feel a bit tired but calm. You feel you have coped well with the situation.

Coping Strategies for the Non-phobic Dental Client

Even if you are not bothered by the thought or action associated with a dental appointment, at the very least, the prospect does upset your typical daily routine. In an already stressed out world some simple guidelines will minimize possibilities that dental care will raise anxiety levels further. With a more than adequate supply of dental personnel in most urban and rural areas, today's care consumer has appointment options well beyond what was common only a few decades ago. Many group practices have hours extending from as early as seven o'clock in the morning to as late as ten o'clock in the evening, five or six days of the week. In larger urban areas it is common to find dental offices that are open weekends.

With such extended hours available to you, choose a day of the week and time of the day that fit comfortably into your schedule. If you don't like driving in rush hour chaos or standing on packed public transit vehicles, choose an appointment time when traffic is lighter. You might be diabetic or suffer from arthritis or some other medical condition that requires medication. Ask for an appointment at a time of day when your medication has taken effect and you are generally feeling your best.

Make sure you are well rested before facing your appointment. Even minor incidents can seem like major crises when you are short of sleep. Set out for your appointment with time to spare. You will be more relaxed upon arrival if you are slightly early than if you have been sitting in traffic watching the minutes slip by. That may give you time to catch up on some reading while in the reception area.

Choose practitioners to whom you can relate well. You should have confidence in your dental staff and feel they are competent in the services they provide to you. You should also like and respect them as people. In a pleasant and non-confrontational manner, let them know what stresses you about dental treatment. Practitioners do understand that more relaxed clients make for more relaxed working environments and better treatment outcomes. Your dental team will appreciate your honesty.

Options for Pain and Anxiety Control

Many dental practitioners have encountered clients whose oral pain has finally outweighed their debilitating fear and driven them to seek emergency care. Dentists will also tell you that providing treatment for people in physical and psychological pain is not easy for either client or practitioner. Modern pharmacological options for pain and anxiety management are available to assist in these situations.

Although dental phobics may have complex dental problems that need to be dealt with in the short term using a variety of "heavy duty" chemical management techniques, the goal is always to help them cope with on-going care needs comfortably with minimal administration of medication.

Pharmacological Pain Control

Oral Sedative Agents

This type of sedation is usually achieved by administration of tablets 30 to 60 minutes prior to the appointment. Commonly used substances include: secobarbital sodium (Secanol); chlorodiazepoxide HCL (Librium) and diazepam (Valium). Since these agents typically cause drowsiness, you should not drive or operate other types of machinery while under their influence. This level of sedation usually involves a sense of euphoria as well as reduction in pain. Since there is no loss of consciousness, you are able to understand information and respond to directions given by your practitioners. Administration of local anaesthetic is used to control pain at the operative site.

Inhaled Sedative Agents

The most commonly used agents in dentistry are nitrous oxide gas in combination with oxygen. These gases control anxiety creating a feeling of relaxation and reduced pain perception. For adequate pain control during the procedure, local anaesthesia will still be required. The gases are delivered through a nose piece worn during the appointment. Effects are realized almost immediately. Rapid recovery and low incidence of side effects make this form of sedation popular among anxious dental clients and their practitioners.

During administration of nitrous oxide you are likely to experience a feeling of warmth and a tingling sensation in fingers and toes. Like other forms of conscious sedation you will remain aware of your surroundings and in control of your actions.

Although nitrous-oxide sedation can be an option for almost everyone, there are some cautions regarding its use as listed below:

▶ *Pregnancy* – although there is no hard evidence that it does harm the fetus, it usually is not administered until after the first trimester of the pregnancy and only with permission of your obstetrician.

▶ *Nasal obstruction* – since the gases are administered through a nose piece, temporary or chronic nasal obstruction can diminish delivery of the drug making its effects unreliable.

▶ *Emphysema, asthma, cystic fibrosis and multiple sclerosis* – these conditions cause breathing difficulties which interfere with safe and effective administration.

Intravenous Sedation

Intravenous conscious sedation involves a minimally depressed level of consciousness. Your vital signs and reflexes will remain and you will still be able to respond appropriately to physical and verbal cues. As with all types of conscious sedation, local anaesthesia will provide pain management at the operative site.

The sedative agent will be dripped into the bloodstream continuously during the procedure. Throughout the appointment and recovery phase a registered nurse will assist in administering the agent and monitoring your response. A third team member, the dental assistant will assist the dentist with the actual procedure.

Oral treatment procedures using conscious sedation techniques are routinely carried out in the dental office. If you are scheduled for treatment under conscious sedation techniques someone must accompany you to the appointment and drive you home.

General Anaesthesia

General anaesthesia can best be described as a controlled state of unconsciousness during which there is a loss of protective reflexes (swallowing, gagging, maintenance of the airway to the lungs, etc.) You will not be aware of, or able to respond to, physical stimulation or verbal commands.

A number of intravenous agents (thiopental sodium, methohexital sodium, etc.) and gases (nitrous oxide – oxygen, halothane, enflurane, etc.) in various combinations can be used to achieve general anaesthesia.
If you need general anaesthesia or if you have health conditions requiring additional

monitoring of any of the techniques described above, the dentist or surgeon is likely to request the use of hospital facilities for the procedures.

Preparing a Child for Professional Dental Care

Correctly preparing a child for professional dental care is probably the most important step in preventing dental phobia. If you take to heart and to hand the home care advice for your child (*Chapter 11*) and have chosen a suitable dental team (*Chapter 2*), the first and future dental visits should be a breeze.

A child's world is full of firsts. Although children usually cope better with some clues regarding what to expect, it is important not to provide excessive information. You might not be representing accurately what will occur and often too much emphasis on the new event can raise suspicion.

In offices where preventive dentistry is practised optimally, your child's first few visits are informal and should occur around his/her first birthday. The youngster simply accompanies an adult or older sibling for a short period of time.

These short visits allow children to experience the sights, sounds, odours and personnel. When they are old enough for professional dental care, these aspects of the office, although not consciously remembered, will not seem strange. The children will already be more at ease when some of the stimuli of the environment are already familiar. By age two to three years, the dental team will want to begin seeing children as clients in order to begin appropriate professional care.

When the child is very young, first professional visits will probably be restricted to quick visual examinations. The child can usually be best handled when sitting on a parent's lap in the dental chair. Once children are comfortable with these procedures, they can begin interacting with the dental team members on their own while mom and dad wait in the reception area. The age at which this occurs varies with each child. Parents however should encourage the child to interact with the dental team directly.

When good dental hygiene is practised and there are no evident problems, a visual exam will suffice until children are four to five years of age. By this time, if a positive rapport has developed, children can usually be seen alone by the dentist or hygienist.

Policies regarding a parent's presence in the dental treatment area vary from practitioner to practitioner. Some work with a welcoming "open door" policy while some suggest the parent be present under certain circumstances. A discussion with the dentist will clarify the existing policy.

If you have confidence in your dental team and encourage your child to grow towards independence, you and your child may not want to remain together during treatment. If your child is shy or has had health problems requiring frequent professional intervention, your presence in the treatment area may be best.

If you remain in the treatment room, you and your child must understand that for the health and safety of all concerned, the professional is in charge. Parents should be prepared to be a stabilizing and reassuring presence.

Often children will play on the parents' protective instincts and overexaggerate negative reactions to treatment. Their prime motives are to gain sympathy or manipulate the situation for promised rewards. Every office staff has witnessed drama kings and queens in action. Parents, rest assured that the dental team, like you, wants the best outcome for your child.

If a visual examination indicates your very young child has already experienced significant disease or an accident has caused physical trauma, your dentist may recommend services of a specialist. Young children with serious dental decay or oral injuries are usually treated in specialty offices or hospital settings where conscious sedation or general anaesthesia can be used. The aim is to accomplish the required treatment in the fewest number of visits with the minimum of psychological trauma. General anaesthesia, although not without risks, provides optimal operating conditions for the dental team. Some conscious sedation techniques and general anaesthesia leave the child with no memories of the extensive procedures performed.

"Behaviour Modeling" to Prepare a Child for Dental Care

Some parents and practitioners feel that hesitant children can benefit from observing dental treatment provided to someone else before they experience the care. Some parents feel that it will be helpful for their child to observe an adult or older sibling being treated. In suggesting or insisting on this, they may be doing their shy child a disservice. Often these parents were frightened in the treatment setting as children. They may still be somewhat apprehensive. To their credit they are interested in trying to prevent their child from becoming fearful. Children, however, are very aware of non-verbal cues and may sense the parent is ill at ease when the parent does not realize s/he is giving off those signals.

Treatment provided to an adult is usually quite different from that for a young child, especially at a child's first visit. Unfortunately, parents do not always realize children can't sort out these differences.

If there is significant sibling rivalry or competition between the older and younger child, having the older child act as a model may not be helpful to the younger one. To insist an older child act as the model for a younger sibling may further complicate the relationship between them.

If your child is very hesitant about receiving treatment and neither you nor the practitioner wants to resort to chemical management techniques, behaviour modeling may still be the answer. Some children, however, will not be convinced regardless of the apparent success of the model's performance. If this is the case other management options will be required. Following the suggestions below will help make the modeling session as helpful as possible for the fearful child.

Creating a favourable behaviour modeling situation:

▶   Let the practitioner identify a child in the practice who is known to exhibit positive behaviour during the same treatment that is necessary for your child.

▶   The child selected should be the same gender and close to the same age as the child observing the behaviour.

▶   The child model and his/her parents must give permission for observation of the treatment session.

▶   The dentist will suggest the shy child receive treatment immediately after the opportunity to observe the model.

▶   The observing child should be briefed on behaviour expected during the observation session. S/he is expected to sit quietly and watch without getting in the way of the dental staff. The parent may be invited to sit with the child.

▶   If the child becomes bored by the session (a good sign), s/he should be allowed to leave.

▶   If the child becomes more upset during observation, s/he should be removed from the treatment room as the modeling effort is not working and other arrangements will be necessary to gain co-operation.

Preparing Your Child for a First "Real" Dental Visit

All dental teams prefer to deal with new clients, young or old, at arranged rather than emergency visits. If your dentist encourages you to bring your infant with you for short informal visits when s/he is tiny, count your blessings. This office truly believes in developing a good working relationship with your child and in early oral health maintenance.

Many practitioners feel that first visits should only begin when children are two to three years of age. Some choose to delay professional visits even longer. Older children have a greater possibility that dental disease is already present and they may have fallen under the negative influences of others regarding dental care information. The checklist below outlines some "do"s and "don't"s when preparing your child for this important first visit.

► Choose an appointment time when you and your child can be at your best.

► Advise the child ahead of time that a visit to the dentist is planned.

► Treat the visit as any normal "first" of growing up.

► Answer questions around the event directly but without excessive detail: you cannot know in advance what interventions the dental team may deem appropriate.

► Ensure that you organize your preparation and departure with time to spare. Rushing creates stress and uneasiness around any activity.

► Introduce your child to the members of the dental team as they appear during the appointment and encourage him/her to interact with the team member directly and independently.

► Allow the professional to take the lead role in establishing rapport with the child. Stay in the background and provide a reassuring presence as required.

► Wait to be invited to accompany the child to the treatment room if the professional feels it would be helpful.

► Never make promises to the child regarding what the dental team will or will not do. Treatment decisions should be left to the professionals.

► Never use bribes to encourage good behaviour: your child will continue to manipulate you for greater rewards.

► Never tell a child that dental treatment won't hurt. If you are referring to it as an everyday occurrence the child will not think about it unless you raise the possibility.

► Never tell medical and dental treatment horror stories when children can overhear and become confused and apprehensive.

► Never use dental treatment as a threat to discourage inappropriate behaviour in other settings.

Chapter 2
Choosing a Dental Care Team

In This Chapter

- ► choosing a dental care team for yourself
- ► choosing dental services for your children
- ► what to look for in a dental office
- ► red flags

Choosing a Dental Care Team for Yourself

You knew it was inevitable but now the announcement is official. Your long-time, well-loved dentist is retiring. There are many ways in which dentists divest themselves of established practices. They may advertise, interview and select an associate (usually a new graduate) to begin working at the site. Using this approach, older practitioners tend to choose associates perceived to have similar approaches to dental service provision as themselves. The new practitioner will be encouraged to attract clients to the practice and as the retiring dentist cuts back on hours of work, will begin seeing long-time clients. When this is the scenario, during the period of overlap there may not be discernable changes in philosophies and strategies of care. The moment of radical change may only occur (or perhaps not) with the final departure of the retiring dentist.

A second approach to practice dissolution is outright sale to a new owner. In a letter of introduction of the new practitioner, your dentist will advise you of the sale effective at a specific date. Your practitioner wishes you well and hopes you will remain in the practice with the new dentist. Without a period of overlap, there is little chance to "check out the new guy (or lady)" before requesting services. You are basically "on your own" to assess and determine your desire to continue as a client in the practice under its new ownership.

Bear in mind, when professional practices (of any kind) change hands you are not a commodity that is simply a part of the sale contract. You are not required to maintain your association with the new owner. Although professionals are famous for referring to "their" clients, they don't own the people for whom they routinely provide service. You are always in the driver's seat. If at any time during your professional association you are unhappy with the service provided, feel free to discuss the matter with your practitioner. If frank, honest, non-confrontational discussion does not improve the situation, always remember: if you have the right to choose continued association with the practitioner you also have the right to end that association.

Perhaps you have relocated for school or work. Whatever the reason, you must find a new dentist. At times this job can seem daunting. The best time to begin the search is before you need emergency assistance. You are in a better position to make workable decisions when you are not in pain. Where to start?

There are a number of strategies you can employ in choosing a new dental team. Probably the most useful is referral from a source you know and trust. Occasionally your former dentist may know practitioners in your new location and may provide a referral.

When you have become acquainted with longer-term residents (neighbours, classmates, co-workers) ask them for suggestions. The more closely their lifestyle mirrors yours, (age, gender, marital status, etc.) the more likely they are to have suggestions which will be helpful. If they have established a comfortable long-term relationship with a dental care team they will usually tell you. Request their permission to use their names when you contact their practitioner as a new client. Dental offices usually welcome new clients referred from established ones.

Most urban centres have local dental societies or study clubs. These organizations are made up of dental professionals (dentists or dental hygienists). They provide a framework for members' professional development and continuing education. Membership in these groups is voluntary. In addition to serving the members, local dental societies often incorporate community service into their mandates.

Many dental societies are listed in the telephone directory. They are usually named for the town or city in which the practitioners are located. If you are living in a city called "Urbania" try looking under "Urbania Dental Society" or "Urbania Dental Hygienists' Society". Depending on the size of the organization there may be full- or part-time staff to answer the telephone and deal with your inquiries. The staff can provide you with a list of practitioners in the area who are accepting new clients. Information about the offices will be restricted to geographical location and type of practice (general or specialty). The staff cannot recommend a specific practice or advise you regarding the character or competence of individual members of the society. When staff members are not in the office a voice-mail service can provide contact information for dentists receiving new clients. Some cities also list a "dental emergency" number in the white pages where a taped message lists dentists on call to provide emergency service.

If you are living in a rural area or a small town, the provincial or state professional association can often provide information. Like professional societies, these organizations are usually named according to their locations, e.g. Ontario Dental Association or Washington Dental Hygienists' Association.

Probably the least desirable strategy for choosing a new dental practice is the cold canvass: using the Yellow Pages of the local phone directory, mapping out a geographical area that is most accessible to you (if it is a large urban centre), and making calls to the offices listed to determine if they are accepting new clients. If they are, you must then determine from your interaction with the receptionist answering the call if the practice is attractive to you.

Choosing Dental Services for Your Children

You grew up with your family dentist and your care has been a series of positive experiences. Your dentist saw you through your pregnancy and expressed interest in pictures of your infant. Now two years later when you want the same positive rapport for your child you are mystified that your dentist suggests you take him to another practitioner. Respect your dentist's recommendation.

When you were a child your dentist was much younger too. As s/he has seen the young children in the practice grow and mature, small children may represent a decreasing percentage of the client pool. Your older dentist may now feel s/he doesn't have the patience to treat children. Be thankful that s/he has been so honest with you. It is all right to be a two-dentist family! Your dentist may even have specific practitioners in mind and will facilitate your acceptance into one of the recommended offices.

If your child is physically healthy and emotionally well-adjusted, a general practitioner who welcomes young children will probably provide suitable care. Many of these dentists are young and sometimes female. When a dentist specifically invites a high percentage of young clients to join the practice, all members of the team are carefully selected for their desire to deal effectively with children's needs.

If your child has serious physical, developmental or emotional challenges, a pediatric specialist is probably a better choice. Like pediatricians, pediatric dentists gear their whole practice philosophy and activity around serving the broadest spectrum of childhood dental treatment needs. By mid-teen years your child will outgrow the services of a pediatric specialist and can become a client in an adult general practice.

What to Look for in a Dental Office

The days of self-sufficiency are long gone. In a world of increasingly specialized services, consumers have to trust that the work done is necessary and properly executed. So it is when you seek dental care. Unless you are a member of the profession, you will not be able to judge the quality of oral care directly. However, there are some signs to look for when visiting an office for the first time. It doesn't always follow but, generally speaking, practitioners who pay attention to details in the physical and social environment of the office pay attention to details in the treatment they provide.

Most medical surgeons do not expect to provide your treatment at a first meeting. They do expect to consult with you, review your condition, perform examinations and discuss proposed treatment options. If you accept service from that practitioner, treatment appointments are arranged. Amazingly, most dental practitioners still expect you to accept some level of treatment (usually your teeth cleaned by the hygienist) at your first appointment.

This philosophy is rather like a car dealership expecting you to buy a vehicle without offering you a test drive. If you are comfortable with this mode of operation, then by all means follow through. If you are not, ask that the first appointment be restricted to meeting the staff, having your needs assessed and treatment proposed. Do expect to pay for the services provided at the assessment appointment at the time it occurs whether or not you decide to continue with the practice to provide further treatment. Any practice that will not agree to this level of service at a first appointment is probably one in which you will not be happy.

If you are a considerate consumer of dental care, i.e. you respect your practitioners by being on time for scheduled appointments, maintaining a helpful attitude during treatment and paying your bills punctually, you will be a welcome addition in any office. Considerate clients have a right to expect consideration in return. Remember, you are choosing the professional. If you suspect at initial contact that the office is not going to respect and appreciate your consideration, then move on.

If you would like some help in making useful observations to aid in your selection of a suitable dental practice, refer to the charts found later in this chapter.

The tables list some common situations new clients might experience during contact with a dental office. Statements on the left are positive, those on the right, less desirable. Note the events that occur during your various office contacts. Add descriptions of other situations as they occur and decide whether these additional items affected you positively or negatively. At the end of your investigation consider the pros and cons you have recorded for each office investigated. You will probably conclude that the office with the best track record of positive aspects is where you would like to be.

Preliminary Contact – The First Phone Call

Your assessment of suitability of a new dental team begins with your first contact with the office. This is usually in the form of a telephone conversation with the receptionist.

Table 2.1 The First Telephone Contact with a Dental Office	
Use the following checklist to record the events and impressions you had from your first telephone contact with a new dental office. Courtesy at a reception desk usually indicates a client at the desk takes priority of service over an in-coming call.	
The telephone was answered (either in person or with a suitable recorded message) after three rings or fewer.	The telephone rang several times before it was answered.
The receptionist confirmed the name of the office and introduced him/herself.	The receptionist did not confirm the office name and/or introduce him/herself.
The receptionist spoke clearly and slowly enough that all information presented was understood.	The message was conveyed so rapidly that you were not sure you had contacted the correct office.
The receptionist advised that a client was at the desk and requested to put you on hold or return your call within a specified short period of time. S/he waited for your response before putting you on hold or taking your number.	The office was identified and you were asked to "hold please" followed by call holding action before you had time to respond.
You agreed to hold the line. The receptionist talked to you every minute or so to advise you on progress towards giving you full attention.	The office was **not** identified and you were asked to "hold please" followed by call holding action before you had time to respond.
You requested a call back as offered and the call was placed within the time frame agreed.	You are left on hold for more than two minutes without contact with the receptionist.
When you were contacted, you felt the receptionist was giving your call his/her undivided attention.	When the receptionist came back on the line you felt s/he was distracted and trying to deal with you and some other job at the same time.
The voice conveyed sincerity, interest, helpfulness and warmth.	The voice conveyed impatience, boredom or inattention.
Information you provided was understood the first time and repeated back to you to verify accuracy of understanding.	You were asked more than once to repeat information you were providing. The receptionist did not verify accuracy.
You asked that the first appointment be for examination only. This was arranged or the receptionist explained this was not routine but would check with the dentist and advise you of his/her answer at a specifically determined convenient time.	You asked for an examination only first appointment and were advised that all new clients had their teeth cleaned before the doctor completed examinations. No other options were presented.
The receptionist asked for your appointment time preferences before offering options.	Appointment times were offered without determining your preferences.
You were invited to ask other questions before the call was completed.	You were not invited to ask for further information.

The First Office Visit

Your assessment of suitability of a new dental team continues with your first on-site visit to the office.

Table 2.2 The First Visit to a Dental Office	
Use the following checklist to record the events and impressions you had of your first on-site contact with a new dental office.	
The receptionist acknowledges your entry with eye contact, pleasant facial expression and, if not on the phone, verbal greeting.	The receptionist whether on the phone or not, does not acknowledge your entry into the office.
As soon as possible, you are invited to approach the desk where the receptionist introduces him/herself.	The receptionist waits until you approach the desk and does not introduce him/herself.
If the office has experienced a schedule adjustment that affects your appointment time, you are advised of this and offered options.	Your appointment will be delayed due to arrival of an emergency client a few minutes earlier but you are not informed of the delay.
The receptionist asks you to fill in paper work and provides the forms on a writing surface and a pen.	The receptionist asks you to fill in forms but does not provide a writing surface and does not offer you a pen.
The receptionist receives the completed forms from your hand and places them where they cannot be seen by other clients at the desk.	The receptionist motions you to place your completed forms on the counter top and retrieves them some minutes later.
When you hand in your forms you are advised that the dentist is running on time or is delayed and invited to take a seat until your appointment time. If a delay is expected, you are advised and given options.	No information is provided on whether your appointment will begin on time.
The reception room is clean, tidy, lit sufficiently for easy vision and pleasantly decorated.	The reception room is untidy, walls marred, furniture in poor repair, lamps inadequate for easy vision.
Literature (professional information, reading material) is up-to-date and neatly and conveniently displayed.	Reading material is out-of-date, tattered and littered about the room.
The dental staff member who appears to take you to the treatment area is clean, neat, hair under control.	The dental staff member who greets you looks unkempt with soiled uniform, shoes, hair falling over face or shoulders.
Staff member is **not wearing operating gloves and/or face mask**.	The staff member **is wearing operating gloves and/or has face mask dangling around his/her neck**.
The staff member calls you by preferred title and surname or title and full name.	The staff member calls you by first name only.
The staff member greets you pleasantly and introduces him/herself and identifies his/her position in the office.	The staff member does not greet you or introduce him/herself or advise of his/her role in the office.

While escorting you to the treatment room the staff member makes pleasant conversation.	The staff member is silent while escorting you to the treatment room.
Public spaces in the office display proof of professional qualifications of the office staff.	There are no professional qualification documents for office staff visible in the public areas of the office.

Assessing the Treatment Room

Dental offices must adhere to rigorous standards to prevent passing diseases from one client to another. Make some basic observations to verify that the office is concerned about infection control.

Table 2.3 Assessing the Treatment Room	
Use the following checklist to record the impressions you had of the dental treatment room in the new dental office.	
The floor is uncarpeted and appears clean.	The floor is carpeted.
The walls are painted a colour that cannot mask dirt and appear fresh and clean.	The walls are a colour that does not suggest cleanliness and paint is chipped or scratched.
Decor is sleek, easily cleaned and serviceable.	The room contains excessive furniture, drapes, wall hangings, etc.
Sterile instrument packs are unopened until treatment is initiated	Instruments are already laid out on trays and exposed to view.
The pathway to the dental chair is not cluttered with other furniture or equipment.	You have to dodge equipment or furniture to access the dental chair.
The dental chair is positioned so you can sit easily.	The dental chair is positioned so it is awkward for you to seat yourself.

Red Flags

If you observe any of the following without an obvious reason, you should be a bit cautious about wholehearted endorsement of the office as a source of dental care. If polite questions regarding your observations are met with annoyance or if you do not receive a satisfactory explanation for the situation, your level of suspicion about the quality of care should rise even higher.

Breaches in Currently Accepted Infection Control Procedures

With diseases such as hepatitis (all forms), HIV/AIDS, tuberculosis, etc. on the rise, infection control protocol in dental offices has changed dramatically. To ensure you are protected during treatments watch for indications that the office is practising all reasonable guidelines. If you observe any of the following, be wary and ask questions. Sometimes people just forget. Sometimes staff members are breaking the rules and the dentist is not aware of the breaches.

▶ Dental personnel are outside the treatment rooms wearing operating gloves and masks, handling phones, client charts, etc.

▶ The practitioners when providing care in the treatment room do not wash hands and put on fresh operating gloves in your presence.

▶ Sterile instrument packs required for your treatment are opened before you enter the treatment room.

▶ Your practitioners handle your treatment documents with gloved hands during or after your treatment.

Social Environment of the Office

Take a few minutes to observe the interactions among office staff members and how they generally interact with other clients. If you note any of the following, it may indicate that people are viewed more as income units rather than personalities to be respected and appreciated.

▶ The pace of the office seems to be generally rushed.

▶ You feel guilty asking a question because the staff is so busy.

▶ Your question is answered but during the interaction the verbal and non-verbal actions of the practitioner make you feel you are imposing.

▶ The staff members seem rushed and impersonal in their interactions with one another.

▶ There is a lack of courtesy displayed among staff members.

▶ The practitioner leaves the treatment room during your appointment without excusing him/herself.

▶ The staff members carry on conversations during your treatment as if you were not there.

▶ Staff members gossip about other clients. If they do this about others, they may feel it is all right to do so about you.

▶ You get the feeling the office is not staffed by people happy with their work environment.

▶ A disparity between what staff members are saying and their facial expressions or body language makes you feel they are insincere.

Part II

What's So Special about Dental Specialties?

Chapter 3

Orthodontics – Straight Talk about Crooked Teeth

In This Chapter

- ► occlusion defined
- ► causes of malocclusion
- ► oral habits and how to correct them
- ► what is orthodontics?
- ► orthodontic biomechanics
- ► treatment options
- ► what to expect during appointments
- ► "invisible" braces

Occlusion Defined

Occlusion is the technical term for the way the upper and lower teeth meet. When the facial bones, muscles and tooth placement in the arches all function harmoniously, the chewing surfaces intermesh with peak efficiency. When any factors act to create less than ideal chewing function, the result is called malocclusion.

Causes of Malocclusion

Studies indicate that, in North America, the incidence of malocclusion runs as high as 95 percent. Crooked teeth are caused by the following factors, acting individually or in combination:

- ► heredity
- ► local factors
- ► facial muscle imbalance
- ► oral habits (see *page 29*)

More specific information on each of these causes will be discussed in turn.

Heredity

Inherited factors are, by far, the most common cause of malocclusion. Each individual is a product of a unique gene pool. As far as dental development is concerned, genes control:

► size and shape of individual teeth

► size, shape and relationship of the dental arches

► presence or absence of teeth (some people have congenitally missing teeth, i.e. teeth that never form)

► presence of extra teeth (some individuals may have more than the normal number of teeth)

► rate of tooth development at all stages

► timing of and growth rate in general and of the face in particular.

When so many factors contribute to the development of a beautiful smile, it is not unusual for some things to go wrong. Slight incompatibilities among the factors can lead to a less than perfect result.

Local Factors

Local factors affecting the development of malocclusion are usually considered to be aspects of the environment of the mouth. These factors include:

► premature loss of baby teeth. When primary teeth are lost early and the permanent replacement tooth is not ready to come into the mouth in its place, space loss occurs in the dental arch. When the permanent tooth is ready to erupt it may be forced out of position due to lack of space.

► prolonged retention of baby teeth. Sometimes the primary tooth roots are not resorbed properly. When these teeth are retained beyond their normal shedding time, they can force the permanent teeth to enter the mouth out of position.

► congenitally absent teeth. In other words, a tooth or teeth just did not form. When tooth units are missing, the remaining teeth will tip or drift in the arch.

▶ existence of extra teeth. Some individuals have extra teeth. These teeth may make their way into the mouth or remain under the gums. Either way, their presence can have an effect on the placement of the normal teeth in the dentition.

Facial Muscle Imbalance

Properly functioning facial muscles are important to the development of the bones of the face and jaws. Individuals who have abnormally functioning facial muscles are likely to develop malocclusion as a result. Facial muscle problems are associated with a variety of hereditary diseases and acquired conditions. These include: Down's syndrome, muscular dystrophy and cerebral palsy.

As with other abnormal muscle use (sucking behaviours and tongue thrust), correction of the malocclusion may not be advisable unless and until the muscle function can be improved. Your medical and dental professionals will need to work closely together to determine if and when orthodontic correction will be beneficial.

For additional information on the classification and development of occlusion please see *Chapter 7*.

Oral Habits and How to Correct Them

Many people know that thumb sucking can cause crooked teeth. It is just one factor which plays a role. Oral habits are major influences on the development of the dentition. Three of these are:

▶ non-nutritional sucking habits
▶ deviant swallowing patterns or "tongue thrust"
▶ chronic mouth breathing

Non-nutritional Sucking Habits

All children are born with a sucking reflex to get food. Some children persist in sucking even when nourishment is not the incentive or the reward. According to Freud's theory of psychosocial development, everyone passes through the "oral phase". At this stage, the mouth is the primary source of sensual pleasure and satisfaction.

To sustain this pleasure the infant or child may choose to suck a bottle, soother, blanket or part of the hand (thumb or finger). Some children adopt such habits and others do not. Possible explanations of why some do, include too early weaning or inadequate nursing time. In the development of malocclusion, the characteristics of sucking habits deserve attention.

Two factors are important:

▶ The longer the habit persists, the greater the chance of permanent change in the occlusion. This is especially true if the habit continues into the mixed dentition phase of development (the time during which some baby teeth and some permanent teeth are present in the mouth).

▶ The intensity of the habit: some children exert very little pressure on the oral tissues when displaying non-nutritional sucking behaviours. Those who exert significant pressure are at greater risk for malocclusion.

If a newborn does not demonstrate a tendency towards non-nutritional sucking there is no need to encourage him/her to use a soother if it is not immediately appealing. Remember that prolonged use of even the best-designed soother can still pose some risk of malocclusion. It is also possible that children who learn to associate psychological comfort with oral stimulation may, later in life, substitute oral behaviours such as smoking or overeating to reduce stress. Such behaviours bring associated problems.

A newborn may indicate a tendency for non-nutritional oral stimulation by sucking of a finger, thumb or blanket. Usually, this will happen at a very early age – several hours or a few days after birth. S/he might have been doing it prior to birth. Rather than discouraging the habit, try to substitute the infant's choice with a suitably designed soother or pacifier. At first the infant may resist the change of device. Be somewhat persistent. When the time comes for the child to outgrow the habit, it will be easier to part with a soother than to give up a thumb- or finger-sucking habit.

The good news is that most children who have used a soother rarely substitute anything else, such as a thumb or finger. Children who have developed a habit of thumb or finger sucking usually have a more difficult time giving up the habit. Their hands are there as a constant temptation to continue to do what they have found comforting.

Ideally a child should be discouraged from a non-nutritional sucking habit between 12 and 18 months of age. By this time the baby is learning to walk, talk and eat. Drinking from a cup accompanies the arrival of solid food in the diet. Even little ones of this age can pattern behaviour after adults. If the decision is made that big boy or girl behaviour does not include using a soother, the child may be quite willing to discontinue its use. If not, don't make an issue of it, but raise the question again a few weeks down the road. Often, once gone, the soother may not be missed. It may just take a day or two of reminding the child what was decided.

If by two years of age, the child is not ready to abandon a sucking habit, the next opportunity of influence may not occur for some years. Two-year-olds have very egocentric views of the world. They are typically impervious to appeals to abide by others' points of view. They favour acting according to their own ideas. Trying to discourage a sucking habit at this time may lead to a contest of wills. Rest assured the child will win. Better wait until the four- or five-year-old begins nursery school or play group and try again. Even at this age, children may be more willing to give up a soother than a thumb or finger.

Try convincing a prekindergarten child that school is a busy place. No time for sucking thumb or soother. Suggest the child practise getting ready for school by abandoning the soother or thumb habit. Some children may be willing to quit cold turkey. For others gradually reducing the availability of the soother will work well.

For children with a thumb or finger habit, reminders may be necessary. With the child's acceptance an adult may become the coach to discourage the sucking habit. Other devices and strategies can work as reminders. **Never use a reminder unless the child sees it as such and agrees to its use. If the child interprets reminders (verbal or otherwise) as harassment or punishment for the habit, that attitude will not help attain the goal.**

Strategies which may work as reminders:

▶ Paint the thumb or finger with a flavour preparation the child does not like (onion, Tabasco sauce, etc.) Commercial products are also available.

▶ Wrap surgical tape around the thumb or finger at times when the child is more likely to suck. Change it often so it remains as clean as possible and maintains the health of the skin underneath it.

▶ Make a cover for the digit, using fuzzy fabric or yarn, which can be tied in place.

▶ Wrap an elastic bandage over the elbow joint of the child's arm just snugly enough that when flexed to put the thumb into the mouth the tension will act as a reminder not to do so.

Many children willing to give up the habit will gain control during the day quite readily. However, for most children, comfort is derived from sucking habits when they are tired, stressed or about to fall asleep. Persistent use of the reminder which has worked best during the day is needed at bedtime until the child can resist the temptation to suck even when partially asleep.

Some children persist in sucking habits until they are preteens or teenagers. By this time, whatever detrimental effect has occurred to the dentition will be permanent. If at this stage orthodontic intervention has been decided upon by parent(s) and child, the sucking habit should be eliminated before treatment begins. At this age children can understand the necessity for discontinuing the habit and are better able to accept assistance in modifying their own behaviour.

If reminders discussed above are insufficient, the orthodontist can fabricate a variety of intra-oral appliances to act as habit breakers. Some of these are removable and some are fixed in place. As with any device, acceptance of its use by the child is important for a successful outcome.

Deviant Swallowing Patterns or "Tongue Thrust"

This is the second type of oral habit which can lead to development of malocclusion. During swallowing, the tongue normally arches from the surfaces of the upper front teeth backward against the palate.

A tongue-thrust habit occurs when the tongue, during swallowing, comes forward between the biting edges of the upper and lower teeth. Breast-fed infants rarely develop this habit. Infants learn this tongue behaviour when bottle-fed with a nipple that has too large an opening. The tongue is used to block the flow of fluid until it can be swallowed. Once the habit is established, this pattern of swallowing occurs consistently.

Since swallowing occurs hundreds of times in a day, this protrusive movement of the tongue keeps the erupting teeth from establishing their normal positions in the arch. The incisors (front teeth) usually are splayed (spread with spaces between them) and tilted towards the lips as a result of the persistent abnormal tongue pressure. The longer the habit persists, the more severe the resulting malocclusion.

Abnormal swallowing patterns can be improved using appliances placed in the mouth and/or *myofunctional* or "muscle function" therapy which teaches the child correct tongue positioning during swallowing. The goal of these interventions is to retrain the tongue to adopt more normal positions at rest and during swallowing.

Orthodontic correction of the malocclusion should be postponed until the oral habit contributing to it is resolved. As long as abnormal oral habits are present, relapse of the malocclusion is likely and, with it, additional stress on the supporting periodontal tissues.

Chronic Mouth Breathing

Children with persistent nasal obstruction (from anatomical deviations, allergies, enlarged adenoids, recurring upper airway infections, etc.) may develop malocclusions if it continues for months or years during facial development.

Individuals who breathe comfortably through their noses carry their tongues at rest, against their palates. Tongue and cheek forces are in balance and normal upper arch width is maintained. With nasal obstruction individuals are forced to breathe through their mouths. To do so, the tongue moves to the floor of the mouth. With the tongue routinely in this position, the cheek muscles, over time, may cause the upper arch to develop narrower than the lower arch.

If this happens, the teeth at the sides and back of the arch may occlude in crossbite. For an explanation of crossbites, please see *Chapter 7*. With narrowing of the arch, some length is lost. Lost arch length may contribute to crowding as the permanent teeth emerge into the mouth.

Oral development in young children with chronic nasal obstructions should be monitored carefully. Orthodontic intervention with either fixed or removable appliances to maintain or regain normal upper arch width can help prevent or reduce the severity of a developing malocclusion.

What is Orthodontics?

By definition, orthodontics is the dental specialty that deals with the prevention, diagnosis and correction of malocclusions or crooked teeth.

Few people are lucky enough to have naturally perfect dentitions. For many, minor imperfections in the dental arches leave the occlusion functional and the appearance pleasing and a bit individualistic. Some severe malocclusions are not only dysfunctional but because they are considered to be unsightly, can also create serious psychological problems.

Serious malocclusions can have any or all of the following effects:

▶ chewing difficulty causing reduced nutrition due to poor food choices
▶ development of abnormal speech patterns
▶ increased risk of oral disease as crooked teeth are more difficult to keep clean
▶ lower self-confidence caused by an unattractive smile.

Although the majority of people seek orthodontic help because they do not like the look of their teeth, the principal aim of treatment is to improve oral health and function in all of its aspects. Fortunately, improved function and improved appearance tend to coincide.

Orthodontic Biomechanics

Simply stated, this is just the process of moving teeth. The physiological processes involved are rather complex. Teeth are supported in the jaw by alveolar bone which surrounds the root. Between the tooth root and the bone is a band of flexible tissue called the periodontal ligament. For a refresher on the structure and function of these tissues please see *Chapter 7*.

Applying pressure to a tooth stretches the ligament on the side of the force and collapses it on the side away from the force. The ligament in an attempt to restore its resting position creates additional bone on the stretched side and removes bone on the collapsed side. This reaction takes place at a cellular level. In this manner, a tooth can be repositioned within the bone. Needless to say, this process takes weeks or months to move the tooth to the position required.

The ease with which a tooth moves depends on a number of factors:

▶ the amount of force used (less is better and safer)
▶ the duration of force application (the most efficient is continuous light pressure)
▶ the size of the tooth (single rooted teeth move more easily than those with multiple roots)
▶ the direction in which the tooth has to be moved.

Tissue Response to Tooth Movement

Light forces applied to teeth stimulate changes in the supporting bone. If too much force is used, changes can also occur in the root surface of the tooth. Root damage falls into the following categories:

Micro-resorption: minor cellular damage to the superficial layers of the root. It is typically repaired by specialized cells in the root cementum tissue which forms the root surface.

Progressive resorption: part of the root tip may be affected and the root becomes slightly shorter. This can happen if too much force is used in tooth movement. Teeth which have to be moved longer distances are more susceptible to this damage, even when proper levels of pressure are used.

Idiopathic resorption: serious loss of root length. Some individuals, for reasons unknown, are more susceptible to this type of root damage, even when all necessary precautions have been taken during treatment.

Orthodontic Appliance Systems

Orthodontic appliances are the "hardware" or the "braces" which move teeth. There are many different systems used throughout the world to achieve the same end.

The most basic differences among systems are those which the wearer can remove and those which are fixed to teeth until the dental professional removes them at the end of treatment. Some elements of the appliance system are worn in the mouth (intra-oral appliances) and some are worn externally (extra-oral appliances or "head gear"). More about head gear later.

Intra-oral Appliances

Each part of the appliance system has a specific purpose. The severity of the malocclusion will influence the orthodontist's choice of recommended appliance therapy. There are advantages and disadvantages to wearing both removable and fixed appliances.

Removable appliances are usually less visible in the mouth. Many designs of removable appliances use frameworks that change muscle function and can interfere with speech. Usually speech difficulties can be overcome fairly readily. Being able to remove an appliance makes oral hygiene an easier task. For an example of a removable appliance see figure 3.1.

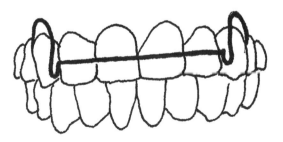

Fig. 3.1A. Hawley removable appliance.　　Fig. 3.1B. Hawley removable appliance in place.

Fixed appliances consist of brackets (and occasionally bands) attached to the teeth. Wires tied into the brackets exert the forces that actually move the teeth. Sometimes, small elastic bands are added to the appliance to facilitate tooth movement. These types of braces usually don't affect speech.

Although the metal bonded brackets are less visible than the old-fashioned bands around each tooth, they are still rather obvious. Clear plastic brackets are a less visible option making only the stainless steel arch wire the most obvious feature of the appliance. Fixed appliances make good oral hygiene a challenge for even the most diligent flosser and brusher. For a closer look at some of these commonly used appliance systems see figure. 3.2.

Fig. 3.2A. Bonded brackets
and arch wire.

Fig. 3.2B. Single
edgewise bracket.

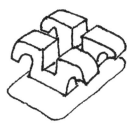

Fig. 3.2C. Double
edgewise bracket.

Extra-oral Appliances

Sometimes malocclusions require correction using anchorage to generate forces that cannot be accommodated using intra-oral appliances alone. Cervical traction devices (head gear) are then used.

These extra-oral appliances consist of a wire framework which attaches to the molar teeth and a strap behind the neck and/or across the top of the head. They are designed to apply force to move teeth or to stabilize teeth that should not be moved.

Since these appliances are highly visible, the good news is, if they are required for treatment, they need only be worn for about 12-14 hours per day. Those hours can usually be accomplished in the privacy of home or in the company of friends. Some examples of head gear can be seen in figure 3.3.

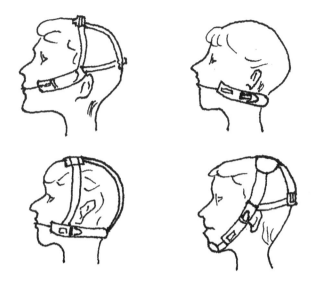

Fig. 3.3. Extra-oral anchorage appliances (head gear).

Treatment Options

Just as in other aspects of dentistry, techniques in orthodontic treatment have changed and improved over the years. Orthodontics was once considered, with rare exceptions, only for children. Today, more and more adults are taking advantage of the improved dental health that treatment can provide. With the development of less visible appliances and dental insurance plans which include subsidy for orthodontics, more adults are encouraged to seek treatment not available to them as children.

Orthodontics has evolved from the process of moving erupted teeth to create a more pleasing appearance to consideration of the harmony of the entire dental-facial complex. Orthodontists can now assess dental and facial growth and its potential. Appliances can be designed to work with growth to encourage it where necessary and to change its direction to create better balance between the teeth and face. Sometimes assessment of the problem dictates that the solution includes removal of teeth that cannot be functionally accommodated within the facial bone structure.

For adults past the point of growth potential, where growth imbalance has left significant oral problems, facial surgery in conjunction with orthodontic tooth movement can greatly improve oral health and function.

To Treat or Not to Treat?

Although most malocclusions benefit from treatment, there are some circumstances that warrant careful consideration before treatment is attempted. Individuals with persistent abnormal muscle reflexes of the cheeks, lips, face and tongue (often associated with an underlying condition such as cerebral palsy) may not benefit in the long run from orthodontic intervention.

Neuromuscular diseases such as muscular dystrophy may cause lack of facial muscle tone. As the dentition works in harmony with normal muscle tone, reduced muscle strength can create difficulties for occlusal function.

Orthodontic treatment, depending on its complexity, may call for years of dedication from the client. During treatment the client is in the driver's seat. No one else can wear or care for appliances as directed. There is little the dental team or family members can do to optimize treatment outcomes if the person wearing the braces is not dedicated to the process. Lack of co-operation during treatment may leave the client with a less functional dentition than if treatment had not been attempted in the first place. This is especially true if correction of the malocclusion required removal of teeth or other surgical interventions.

The central question each orthodontist considers when assessing a client is, "Should this malocclusion be treated?" If s/he concludes there are limitations that suggest an unstable outcome is possible, these risks will be clearly explained.

What to Expect during Appointments

First of all it is important to remember that, to be successful, orthodontic treatment demands commitment from the client. Daily maintenance of good oral hygiene and wearing and caring for appliances are musts.

If treatment involves working with growth factors for optimal results, it may span several years. The time spent will include periods of waiting for growth to occur interspersed with periods of appliance wear. Half-hearted commitment to orthodontic treatment will not result in the best outcome.

Appointment Sequence

When the family dentist spots a problem, s/he is likely to recommend a consultation with an orthodontist and may suggest a number of practitioners from which to choose. When the choice is made, the general practitioner's office may make the initial appointment or suggest the client does so. Orthodontists do not usually arrange consultation appointments for clients without professional referral.

The Initial Consultation

Expect this appointment to be about 45 minutes in length. During this visit, the client's general and dental health histories will be discussed. The orthodontist will also want to know reasons for seeking treatment and the client's previous knowledge about or experience with orthodontics.

With histories recorded, the examinations are undertaken. The facial pattern will be observed, followed by careful examination of teeth and periodontal tissues (gums). An assessment will be made on how the jaw joint functions and how the teeth occlude (bite together).

Upon completion of the examinations the orthodontist will discuss the obvious aspects of the problem and suggest the feasibility of treatment. Fees for this consultation will be payable on completion of the appointment. If a decision is made to begin treatment, two appointments will be arranged. The first to create the records required for a complete diagnosis and the second to discuss the proposed treatment plan. The records and consultation appointments are also billed separately from charges for actual treatment.

The Records Appointment

This appointment takes about one hour. The records required to assess the problem and make treatment decisions are collected. These include:

► photographs
► x-rays
► study models

Photographs: Photographs are taken from full face and profile perspectives. Intra-oral pictures are also taken of the teeth from a number of viewpoints. These pictures serve two purposes: a way to observe details of the malocclusion and a record of the pre-treatment condition. Teeth move slowly. Often clients feel as if treatment is getting nowhere. A quick look back at where things were, confirms progress made and helps keep motivation for treatment high.

X-rays: The standard reason for taking any x-ray is to see what can't be observed any other way. So it is in this case. For orthodontic diagnosis the following radiographs are usually produced:

▶ a panoramic film which is taken from outside the mouth and shows all the teeth

▶ a lateral cephalogram (also taken from outside the mouth) which shows the bones of the face and part of the skull

▶ supplemental intra-oral radiographs (where the film is placed in the mouth) which show specific teeth in greater detail.

Study Casts or Models: These models provide an exact replica of the teeth in each arch and are prepared so that they demonstrate the current occlusion. To make them, trays with a gelatinous paste are pressed over the teeth in each arch. In a short time the paste changes to a rubbery consistency and the material, with its voids, creates a negative image of the structures it covered.

Dental plaster is poured into the imprint and a three dimensional model emerges. These models allow the orthodontist to study the teeth and occlusion in more detail than can be observed when doing an intra-oral examination. In fact, it is the only way of getting a really good view of the teeth in occlusion from the tongue side. The client therefore does not have to wait while the orthodontist takes specific measurements and deliberates on treatment options. Figure 3.4 illustrates a set of orthodontic records models.

Lastly, like the photos, models provide a pre-treatment record for comparison to determine treatment progress.

Fig. 3.4. Orthodontic records models.

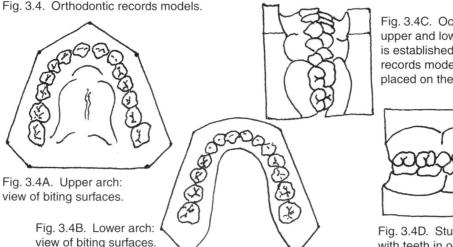

Fig. 3.4A. Upper arch: view of biting surfaces.

Fig. 3.4B. Lower arch: view of biting surfaces.

Fig. 3.4C. Occlusion of upper and lower arches is established when records models are placed on their backs.

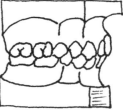

Fig. 3.4D. Study models with teeth in occlusion.

The Consultation

Consultation appointments are usually about one hour in length. They are arranged after the orthodontist has studied the records and determined recommended treatment options. At this time, the orthodontist will use the diagnostic records to explain the nature of the problem. S/he will review the options available in detail and answer any questions regarding the treatment process.

At the end of this meeting it is important that the client and others involved know exactly what to expect during treatment. It is also important for the client to understand the expectations of the practitioners providing the treatment regarding co-operation during the process.

Information discussed at the consultation appointment with the orthodontist should include:

▶   preparation for appliance therapy, i.e. do teeth need to be surgically uncovered, removed or restorations placed prior to treatment? If a referral to an oral surgeon is required, the orthodontist may make some suggestions or suggest you talk to your family dentist about making arrangements for you.

▶   the type of appliance therapy proposed

▶   appointment sequences and time intervals between visits

▶   the time frame in which treatment is likely to be completed.

It is not unusual for another staff member in the office to provide and discuss the following additional information:

▶   cost estimates for the service including portions covered by insurance and payment options for the balance

▶   office policies regarding client co-operation, e.g. how will problems such as not wearing removable appliances; routine poor oral hygiene; undue breakage of appliances, etc., be dealt with by the practitioner?

The decision to accept treatment does not have to be made immediately. Once a decision to proceed is made, the client advises the office receptionist and a series of appointments will be arranged. The sections following describe typical appointments involved in correcting a malocclusion using fixed intra-oral appliances (braces) on both dental arches and an extra-oral head gear appliance to provide anchorage.

Fixed Appliance Options

If the malocclusion is severe enough to require brackets bonded to each tooth, the choice of standard stainless steel or clear plastic is available. Plastic brackets have the advantage of being less visible in the mouth but have the disadvantage of being somewhat more susceptible to wear and tear. This means they may need to be replaced more frequently during the course of treatment than their steel counterparts.

Regardless of bracket choice, arch wires only come in stainless steel. In plastic brackets, the fine wires used at the beginning of treatment are barely visible. As treatment progresses and heavier gauge wires are used, they become more obvious.

Ties used to keep the arch wires in the bracket slots can be made of stainless steel or elastic. Elastic ties come in clear, beige, grey, or a variety of colours.

The Appliance Placement Appointments

Separation/Preparation

Usually when a head gear is anticipated as part of treatment, bands are placed on the upper first molar teeth. Often if the teeth in the arch have very tight contacts between them, it is necessary to create a little space before the bands are fitted. Brackets will be bonded to the remaining teeth in the arches.

There are two ways to bond brackets to teeth. The first method is called *direct* technique and involves preparing the tooth surfaces for the bonding material and then placing the brackets one by one on the teeth.

A second technique, referred to as *indirect*, uses a work model of the arch to set the brackets in the correct alignment. A tray is then formed over the brackets on the model using a rubber-like material to trap the brackets. The tray containing the brackets is then removed from the model. During the bonding process, the tooth surfaces are prepared and the trays are fitted over the arches. Using this technique, all of the brackets are placed on the teeth at once.

If treatment calls for bands and direct bracket placement, a very short appointment is arranged to place separation devices on either side of the teeth to be banded so that space is created between the teeth in that part of the arch. With space around the molars, band fitting and final cementation will be much easier for client and practitioner.

If the orthodontist prefers indirect bond placement, impressions for work models will be taken at the separation placement appointment. The preparation appointment is usually scheduled about one week prior to appliance placement.

Appliance Placement Appointment

This is usually the longest appointment in the sequence – probably about two-and-one-half hours. At the end of this session, teeth are now moving.

During this appointment expect the following:

▶ removal of the separation devices

▶ fitting and cementation of the bands (Dental cement is used between the band and the tooth to fill the gap and prevent the possibility of plaque forming under the band and causing tooth decay.)

▶ bonding of brackets to teeth

▶ placement of arch wires (The arch wires are the major "active" elements of orthodontic appliances. They actually do the work of moving teeth. The bands, tubes, brackets and hooks are simply there to act as sites of attachment for the active parts of the appliance to direct forces on the teeth. Preliminary arch wires are very light gauge and exert gentle forces to initiate tooth movement. As treatment progresses, increasingly heavier gauge wires are used.)

▶ instruction on care of appliances (Oral hygiene has now become more difficult. The office staff will provide tools and suggestions on how best to clean teeth and appliances.)

With the newly placed appliances the soft tissues of cheeks and lips will register the sharp edges. However, the mucosa (the tissue lining the lips and cheeks) will adjust quickly.

In the meantime, the orthodontist will provide a strip of soft wax about the size of a piece of licorice. If the brackets irritate the soft tissue a small piece of wax covering the offending spot for a day or two will bring relief. The wax is meant to be used occasionally for emergency relief. Clean wax should be kept available in case a wire breaks and poses a hazard to soft tissue. Cover the broken area until the problem is fixed.

Active Treatment Appointments

Once all the intra-oral appliances are placed, treatment appointments are scheduled every four to six weeks. At that time, the arch wires will be removed and the bands and bonds checked to ensure they are securely attached. The orthodontist will prescribe a new arch wire which will then be tied in place.

Over time, other active devices may be added. These include coil springs (usually fixed in place) and elastics (usually under client's control). If they are used, instructions on wear and replacement will be given to the client.

When treatment has progressed to the point where increased anchorage is needed, the head gear (extra-oral traction appliance) will be fitted. Clients are usually required to wear head gear at least 12-14 hours a day (around the house and to bed). They must also take the appliance to every treatment appointment so it can be checked and adjusted. Failing to follow instructions will slow treatment progress.

The length of treatment appointments can vary. Although the orthodontist is ultimately in charge of treatment, dental hygienists and dental assistants will probably perform various tasks under his/her direction and supervision. Active treatment appointments usually take about a half hour.

The Red Letter Day – Appliance Removal

The big day has finally arrived. Arch wires come out for the last time. Bands and bonded brackets are removed. Remnants of the cement and bonding material are carefully removed. The client gets to see the results of hard work and patience.

More impressions for models are taken. At least one set is used to create work models for fabrication of retainers. Sometimes a set for is taken to create post-treatment record models. Clients who travel a distance to see the orthodontist are usually provided with "same day" retainer service. The de-banding appointment will be made first thing in the morning and retainers fitted later in the day. Clients living locally may be granted a few days appliance free.

Treatment is not over yet. The retention phase has begun. Retainers will hold teeth in their new positions until the bone, gum tissues and facial muscles get used to the new arrangement. *Failure to wear retainers as directed can result in significant relapse of the malocclusion.*

Upper arch retainers are usually removable. They often consist of a plastic plate which covers part of the roof of the mouth. Wire clasps fit over the first molars to stabilize the retainer. An adjustable front wire curves around the front of the upper anterior teeth (usually canine to canine). It takes practice to learn to talk clearly around a maxillary retainer but it will soon be mastered.

Retainers must be handled carefully so that the facial wire and clasps are not distorted. Retainers need to be cleaned each time teeth are brushed and flossed.

Retainers on the lower teeth may also be removable. Some may consist of a short wire, bent to adapt to the tongue side of the lower front teeth. This wire is bonded in place so it cannot be removed. A floss threader is needed to clean between these teeth under the wire.

After the retention phase is completed, clients need only to wear and care for their new smiles. The orthodontic staff has finished its job and oral health maintenance support reverts to the family dentist.

"Invisible" Braces

Most clients, particularly adults, pondering the question of having their teeth straightened have at least minor concerns about the appearance of the appliances. For some people the thought of living with a "metal mouth" deters them from seeking treatment altogether. For them, information about invisible appliances will be welcome. A brief explanation is warranted.

This system uses a series of clear plastic appliances rather like custom-fitted mouthguards. Once the orthodontist has assessed the client's needs and formulated a treatment plan s/he can determine whether this system can create a favourable result.

If the "invisible" system is recommended, the client will then be appointed for impressions to create models of the teeth. These are sent to the dental lab where a technician sections the model and repositions the teeth slightly moved towards their desired final positions. Using this adjusted model, the plastic appliance is fabricated.

The client returns to the orthodontist where it is checked for fit. At first, some jiggling will be required to coax the teeth into the "abnormal" positions dictated by the appliance. Teeth will move most efficiently if it is worn as much as possible: "24/7" is preferred. Removal makes eating and oral hygiene procedures easy. As the teeth move, inserting and removing the appliance becomes easier.

At the stated appointment interval, the process is repeated and a sequence of appliances will move the teeth to their final locations.

Clients need to be aware of the limitations of this system. It works best when malocclusions are slight and required tooth movements for correction, minor. For example, people may be concerned about minor spacing of their teeth. This system might be an appropriate choice to close the spaces. Some teeth may be slightly tipped or rotated. If there is sufficient space in the arch to accommodate the correction, again this system may be feasible. For significant malocclusions requiring many teeth to be moved considerable distances, the standard fixed appliance therapy may be the best or only option for correction.

Chapter 4

Periodontics

In This Chapter

- ▶ what is periodontics?
- ▶ phases of periodontal treatment
- ▶ treatment options and appointment expectations
- ▶ common periodontal surgical interventions
- ▶ use of antimicrobial chemical agents in periodontal therapy

---

What is Periodontics?

By definition, periodontics is the dental specialty that deals with the diagnosis and treatment of diseases of the supporting tissues of teeth. Where periodontal disease has already destroyed these tissues, surgical techniques can improve appearance of the resulting defects.

The chapters in Part V explain how dental disease is largely preventable. If periodontal disease goes unchecked, it can have numerous negative results. Some of these are listed below:

- ▶ chronic tooth sensitivity to heat and cold caused by gingival recession (loss of gum tissue)

- ▶ chronic halitosis (bad breath)

- ▶ tooth mobility due to irreversible bone loss

- ▶ changes in occlusion (bite) due to migration of teeth from loss of supporting alveolar bone

- ▶ tooth loss (more commonly from periodontal disease than from decay)

- ▶ visible and unsightly soft tissue defects that cause an unattractive smile

- ▶ general bodily (systemic) infection caused by oral bacteria accessing the bloodstream via infected gums

► medical complications from systemic infection for individuals with prosthetic joints, heart valves, or suppressed immune system function.

The main goal of periodontal treatment is to break the cycle of disease and improve the health of all tissues that support teeth. Unfortunately, periodontal disease can cause irreversible tissue loss. Although some surgical techniques can improve the appearance of defects left by disease, there are significant limits to this type of intervention.

Phases of Periodontal Treatment

Sanative Phase

This is the first phase of periodontal treatment. It is the least invasive and fundamental to any further interventions. It is the aspect of treatment that focuses on identifying and removing the elements causing and contributing to the disease. These elements include:

► presence of hard deposits on the teeth (known in the profession as "calculus", more commonly referred to as "tartar")

► presence of organized bacterial plaque or biofilm

► faulty restorations which may lead to plaque retention and food impaction between teeth

► occlusal (biting) factors which may cause unnecessary or unnatural pressures on some of the teeth in the arches

► localized trauma to soft tissues and/or tooth roots caused by aggressive oral hygiene habits (usually improper brushing with hard-bristled toothbrushes and highly abrasive pastes)

► improper use of dental floss or toothpicks

► smoking or use of oral tobacco

► habitual use of any product which causes acid to form and pool against the oral soft tissues, e.g. placing such things as ASA tablets directly on tissue or placing sour candies between the cheeks and teeth and letting them dissolve slowly.

The goal of the sanative phase is to remove or reduce the causative factors and break the disease cycle. For a complete discussion of the oral disease process, please see *Chapter 8.*

Unless the disease potential is reduced to a minimum, complicated further treatment interventions are doomed to fail.

While clinical procedures during the sanative phase are being completed, daily self-care measures designed to regain and maintain oral health are taught to the client. Reassessment of tissue condition after a few months will determine the success of the sanative phase and will dictate whether or not additional treatment is required.

Surgical Phase

If the sanative phase has been successful and the oral tissues are again healthy, surgical interventions may be required to:

► change the shape of hard and soft tissues so that home care procedures to control bacterial plaque build-up are easier (A cleaner mouth on a daily basis reduces the potential for recurrence of disease.)

► stabilize teeth which have lost bone support

► improve appearance.

Each of the procedures listed is explained in some detail later in this chapter. Commonly performed periodontal surgeries include:

► pocket reduction procedures (gingivectomy or gingivoplasty)

► flap surgery to assist in correction of periodontal defects

► soft tissue grafts

► bone grafts

► guided tissue regeneration.

Treatment Options and Appointment Expectations

Referral to a periodontist may occur for the following reasons:

► lack of regular preventive dental treatment that has allowed periodontal disease to progress to a serious state

► mouth tissues have become damaged to the point of needing the attention of a specialist.

If referral is advisable, the general practitioner will recommend a practitioner who will provide care. The referring dentist may arrange the appointment or advise the client to do so.

Initial Consultation

This appointment is usually about 45 minutes in length. During the visit, the client's general and dental health histories are reviewed. The periodontist will also want to discuss the reasons for seeking treatment and what the client already knows about his/her condition.

The periodontist will then conduct a thorough oral examination noting the colour, contour and consistency of all of the oral tissues to determine the extent of disease. Instruments used to probe under the gums will measure the length of the soft tissue flap that lies against the tooth and reveal the presence of hardened deposits. In some cases, bacterial cultures will be taken and analyzed to determine the strains of bacteria present.

If the soft tissue has receded below its normal level on the tooth, these variations will be recorded. Any areas of soft tissue that bleed, either spontaneously or upon use of instruments will be noted since bleeding is a sign of disease. For more information on the periodontal disease process please see *Chapter 8.*

In addition to visual examinations, intra-oral x-rays (exposed with the film in the mouth) will be taken to provide additional information on the health of the supporting bone. These radiographs also help determine if tooth defects or the margins of restorations are contributing to plaque retention and calculus formation.

With the examinations complete the periodontist will discuss the problem and suggest the feasibility of treatment in the short and long terms. Short-term treatment usually concentrates on the goals of the sanative phase and the time line in which it should be completed. Long-term treatment projections assume a positive outcome from the sanative phase. Estimates of a time frame and costs of each phase of service should be provided.

If the treatment proposal is accepted, the office staff will arrange appointments for the sanative phase. They can also provide information regarding the cost of treatment and financial arrangements available.

Sanative Phase Appointments

Removal of hard deposits from deep under the gums may take a single appointment of about an hour to remove them thoroughly. For clients who have not had their teeth professionally cleaned in several years, a series of appointments may be necessary.

These appointments are still usually about an hour in length, but each appointment targets a specific smaller area of the mouth. It may take from two to six appointments to complete the sanative phase. At these appointments, clients are instructed on the best ways to use oral hygiene devices (toothbrushes of various designs, dental floss, toothpicks, etc.) to maintain oral hygiene on a daily basis.

If deposits are heavy, removal procedures are usually done after placement of local anaesthetic in the area. This makes the procedure more comfortable and less stressful for both client and practitioner.

Since the tissues were diseased, some post-operative discomfort as they heal should be expected. Gentle, effective oral hygiene measures in the area are a must and warm salt-water rinses will help both the healing and the discomfort. About 2.5 ml (½ tsp) of table salt in a small glass of comfortably warm water is held in the mouth against the tissues. Rinse and spit out. Repeat several times for a total time of one to two minutes. This is most helpful if done two or three times a day for several days after appointments. Salt water helps reduce swelling, enhances blood flow to the area, is a natural antiseptic and promotes healing.

If restorations are identified as factors contributing to periodontal disease, they will need to be altered by the family dentist. The best time to have this done is a few weeks after completion of the sanative phase of treatment. With the removal of oral deposits and improved soft tissue health, correction of faulty fillings or placement of new restorations can be done more easily with a better final result.

Common Periodontal Surgical Interventions

Pocket Reduction (Gingivectomy or Gingivoplasty)

Information about normal periodontal anatomy can be found in *Chapter 7*. The portion of gum tissue professionally called "free gingiva", when healthy, lies snugly against the necks of the teeth rather like a turtleneck sweater. The depth of this flap from its margin to its attachment should be from 1 mm to 3 mm. When tissues are under attack from disease, this tissue swells and loss of bone at the site of attachment can cause formation of a periodontal pocket. Any area 4 mm or deeper is considered to be a periodontal pocket. For more detailed discussion of periodontal disease and resulting tissue deformities please see *Chapter 8*.

On completion of the sanative phase of treatment, some reduction in pocket depth is expected as tissues heal and swelling resolves. However, if any periodontal pockets measuring 5 mm or more remain, surgery may be indicated to reduce their depth.

Where surgical pocket depth reduction is feasible, two possible techniques are available. In gingivectomy, a portion of the free gingiva is removed to make the pocket shallower. In gingivoplasty, the free gingiva is repositioned to reduce pocket depth but no tissue is removed. Both procedures are performed under local anaesthesia.

Periodontal Flap Surgery

As gory as it may sound, during flap surgery the soft tissue of the gums is carefully moved to expose the underlying bone. This is done for two reasons:

▶ to gain access to the tooth root surface so that all deposits and diseased root material can be removed

▶ to gain access to bony defects caused by disease that has destroyed bone tissue of the socket.

Once the area has been cleaned and the bone recontoured, the soft tissue is sutured back in place. During replacement of the flap the tissue will be positioned so that the pocket depth is reduced to normal measurements.

Soft Tissue Grafts

A quick review of the structure of the periodontal tissues found in *Chapter 7* will be helpful to understand the reasons for soft tissue grafting. As described in that chapter there is a zone of gum tissue between the free gingiva and the linings of the cheek and lips (oral mucosa). This tissue, referred to as attached gingiva, is firmly attached to the underlying bone.

If periodontal disease is allowed to progress in an area, pocket formation and/or gingival recession reduces the width of attached gingiva. If not checked, eventually the zone will be eliminated and pockets will extend to the level of the oral mucosa. To prevent this, soft tissue grafts are performed to increase the zone of attached gingiva in the affected areas.

If the area of defect is small (affecting one or possibly two teeth), attached gingiva may be moved from the margins of the site. The tissue will be surgically repositioned and sutured into place. If the defect or area at risk involves a larger area, donor tissue is required. This tissue may be taken from the client's palate. During this procedure, the recipient site is prepared. A carefully shaped piece of donor tissue is removed from the palate and sutured in the new site.

Some periodontal surgeries may not require a dressing. The client will be instructed on care of the surgical sites until healing is completed.

Some periodontal surgical procedures require the placement of a dressing – the equivalent of a bandage in conventional surgery. Research into wound dressing now allows the use of adhesive tapes to cover a surgical site. This transparent material allows the blood clot to form beneath it. As healing progresses, the tape will loosen and fall off.

Some periodontal dressings are products mixed as pastes and applied to the surgical sites. Once in place, they harden not unlike a plaster cast. They serve to protect the site from food impaction and abrasion. They also contain ingredients which sooth the injured tissues and promote healing. Care should be taken when performing oral self care in areas adjacent to the surgical sites. If dressings are used they are usually removed at one week post-operatively. The periodontist will check the healing process and remove debris and sutures (if indicated) from the surgical sites. If all is well, the dressing is not replaced. Additional instructions are given for self care. If healing has been delayed, a fresh dressing will be placed and rechecked, usually in another week's time.

If there are both a surgical and a tissue donor site, dressings may be placed initially on both. Since donor sites are frequently on the palate and dressing retention is difficult in this area, most practitioners do not expect to find it in place at the one week post-op check. If palatal dressings are lost in a day or two, most doctors do not replace them unless the client has difficulty coping with the exposed area and is willing to make an extra trip to the office for a new dressing. If, however, the dressing on the surgical site is disturbed or lost, it should be reported to the periodontist. Advice will be given regarding assessment and management of the site. This may or may not mean another trip to the office.

Many practitioners will prescribe chemical plaque-control agents (usually in the form of mouthwash) on a temporary basis during recovery from surgery. These products help reduce bacterial levels in the mouth until a thorough daily mechanical plaque-control routine can be resumed.

Bone Grafts

Some defects in alveolar bone caused by periodontal disease can benefit from placement of a bone graft. To be candidates for these procedures, the bony defects must display specific characteristics. Bone grafts are not possible for some types of bone loss. In cases where they are possible, either natural bone or synthetic bone substitute is used to fill the defect. This procedure aims to:

▶ promote growth of new alveolar bone

▶ encourage addition of cementum tissue on the tooth root surface

▶ enhance formation of new fibres in the periodontal ligament.

The procedure involves exposing the bone (flap surgery as described above). The tooth root will be cleaned of deposits and necrotic (dead) tissue. The diseased bone will also be removed. The preferred graft material will be packed into the prepared site and the soft tissue sutured in place. The periodontal dressing will be left in place for seven to 14 days. Upon removal, the site will be cleaned and the client advised of appropriate self-care measures until healing is complete.

Guided Tissue Regeneration

This is the newest and most complicated periodontal surgical technique available. As the name suggests, the goals of this treatment are to:

▶ encourage regeneration of natural healthy tissue in sites where periodontal disease has removed the tissues.

▶ reduce pocket depth

▶ increase the zone of attached gingiva

▶ fill bony defects

▶ regenerate alveolar bone.

This treatment is indicated for only a limited number of types of small defects. It involves surgical preparation of the site and use of synthetic membrane material to stimulate regenerative growth of alveolar bone, root cementum and the periodontal ligament.

The complexities of this surgery are beyond the scope of this book. A periodontist will discuss the procedures in detail with possible candidates for this type of treatment.

Use of Antimicrobial Chemical Agents in Periodontal Therapy

Chapters 10, 11 and *12* discuss a variety of useful daily oral hygiene measures. At this time, long-term chemical control of oral bacteria is not advisable or feasible. There is, however, a role for antimicrobial agents in the surgical treatment of periodontal disease. When used in this manner, the goal of the agent is to reduce the number of disease-producing bacteria during the surgical procedure and healing phase of treatment.

Two types of agents are available. *Antiseptics* are chemicals which kill bacteria on contact or prevent their multiplication. *Antibiotics* are substances which kill other organisms or prevent their multiplication.

The two most serious disadvantages of overuse of antiseptics and antibiotics are:

▶ they often affect the numbers and growth of non-disease-producing or beneficial bacteria in the body

▶ their overuse causes organisms previously affected by them to become resistant to the effects.

Antimicrobial agents are delivered to the body in three different ways: topically; topically in controlled-release format; systemically.

Topical Antimicrobial Agents

Topical application of an agent means it is applied directly to the area or tissue that is to receive the benefit. Oral topical agents are generally in the form of mouthrinses. Mouthrinses are usually categorized as: *therapeutic* (when some health improvement is expected) and *cosmetic* (those formulated to refresh the mouth and change breath odour temporarily).

During periodontal surgical treatment therapeutic mouthrinses may be used to:

▶ reduce the bacteria in the mouth prior to surgery

▶ reduce oral bacterial levels during the healing process post-surgery when mechanical plaque-control techniques require modification or elimination for a period of time.

Mouthrinses are limited in their effectiveness to reducing bacterial populations that exist superficially on the tissues. They will not reach plaque resting in the sulcus (trough) between the free gingiva and the tooth or at the base of periodontal pockets.

Topical agents can be placed in a periodontal pocket using an oral irrigating device (see figure 4.1). The material may be applied by a dental practitioner or by the client after instruction on the procedure. The goal of irrigation is to reduce the bacterial load in the pocket and improve tissue health. To do so a daily application over a defined period of time usually is recommended.

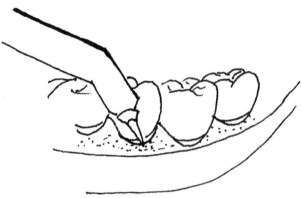

Fig. 4.1. Subgingival irrigation.

Systemic Antibiotics

Occasionally areas of periodontal infection prove resistant to all sanative and topical forms of antibacterial therapy. When this occurs, the periodontist will take a bacterial culture from the infected site and have it analyzed. When the strains of bacteria present are identified, an appropriate systemic antibiotic will be prescribed.

Clients will be placed on a short course of tablets to eliminate the oral infection present. When antibiotics are prescribed it is important to take **all** of the medication as instructed.

Chapter 5
Oral Surgery and Other Specialties

In This Chapter

► oral surgery defined
► scope of practice of oral surgeons
► maxillofacial surgery
► the role of prosthodontists
► endodontic practice
► denturists

Oral Surgery Defined

Dental surgeons, oral surgeons, what's the difference? While it is true that all poodles are dogs and all oral surgeons are dental surgeons, it is also true that not all dogs are poodles and not all dental surgeons are oral surgeons. In the health care field, a surgeon is any practitioner qualified and licensed to cut body tissue. Under this definition a dentist who confines his or her practice to restoring teeth can be referred to correctly as a dental surgeon.

All dental specialists must complete the basic undergraduate program in dentistry before beginning advanced training in their chosen field. A dental surgeon is trained and licensed to cut hard tissues to restore teeth, soft mouth tissues to perform basic periodontal treatment, and to remove teeth. To qualify as an oral surgeon requires a number of years of post-graduate study beyond a degree in dental surgery.

In areas where periodontists and oral surgeons are in short supply, a dentist or dental surgeon will probably perform complex tooth extractions and periodontal procedures more frequently than urban dentists who have the option of referring a client to an easily accessible specialist. The specialty of periodontics is discussed in *Chapter 4*.

Scope of Practice of Oral Surgeons

Most people have heard tales of woe around removal of impacted wisdom teeth. A large percentage of an oral surgeon's practice time is spent in performing difficult tooth extractions. Many urban dentists, although legally qualified to remove teeth from any location in the mouth, prefer to leave complicated extractions to the specialists who do them routinely.

Often a dentist who has recommended full or partial dentures as the treatment of choice will suggest to the client that an oral surgeon extract the multiple teeth that require removal. At that time the surgeon will contour the bone remaining in the dental arch to make fitting of the denture easier. If the treatment of choice is an implant-supported prosthesis (denture), the oral surgeon may be called upon to place the implant devices.

When orthodontists complete specialty education they usually give up restorative practice including tooth removal. If their treatment plans call for multiple tooth extractions to relieve a crowding problem it is usually an oral surgeon who is recommended to remove the teeth. Sometimes in orthodontic treatment, impacted teeth, especially maxillary canines, are uncovered by oral surgeons. During this procedure the soft tissue and bone over the tooth are removed so that the orthodontist can attach an appliance to the tooth to move it into its correct position in the arch.

General dentists who find suspicious oral lesions may refer the client to an oral surgeon for a biopsy procedure. Oral surgeons also remove lesions such as cysts and tumours that if left alone may destroy bones of the face or cause other serious problems. Jaw joint and salivary gland surgeries are also part of the oral surgeon's repertoire.

Clients facing more complex surgical procedures can appreciate not only the oral surgeon's extensive training in surgical techniques but also their ability to use a wider range of options to eliminate pain and reduce anxiety that comes with extensive interventions.

Oral surgeons typically have office suites and personnel available to perform procedures under conscious sedation or general anaesthesia. When clients have underlying medical issues or are facing surgeries that require hospital facilities, oral surgeons have hospital privileges to accommodate these needs.

Maxillofacial Surgery

Practitioners with this capability represent the highest level of specialty education in oral surgery. Their area of expertise lies in facial reconstruction. In conjunction with orthopedic and plastic surgeons, orthodontists and others, they perform sophisticated surgical procedures to:

▶ correct serious, handicapping malocclusions where the root cause is skeletal deficiency of the facial bones

- ▶ improve facial patterns and dental function for individuals born with hereditary problems such as cleft lip and palate

- ▶ repair major facial injuries such as those sustained in a car accident

- ▶ remove extensive benign and malignant tumours and perform the necessary reconstructive procedures.

The Role of Prosthodontists

Prosthodontics is the specialty that deals with replacement of natural teeth with dentures or false teeth. While many dental surgeons routinely provide complete and partial dentures for their clients, occasionally clients are best served by a specialist in the field.

As explained in *Chapter 7*, after teeth are removed, the bone that normally supports them in the mouth is resorbed by the body. Since the bony ridge is required to support removable dentures, as it deteriorates over time, retention of a denture becomes more difficult. Prosthodontists have experience in designing and modifying oral appliances to make them as efficient as possible for clients.

As fewer people are candidates for overdentures and implant-supported appliances (discussed in *Chapter 14*) prosthodontists have wider experience in dealing with these procedures than restorative dentists and are usually called upon to provide these services when required.

Prosthodontists work in partnership with the maxillofacial surgeon, plastic surgeon and others to provide comprehensive client care where prostheses (artificial body parts such as dentures, devices to form an artificial palate in cleft palate cases, etc.) are required in facial reconstruction. It is usually the prosthodontist who designs and co-ordinates construction of the prostheses.

Endodontic Practice

Those of you who have had root canal therapy know about the scope of practice of endodontists. Those of you who have not had this experience – don't believe everything you hear about the dreaded "root canal".

Endodontics refers to the removal of diseased pulp tissue from the centre of teeth when removal of the affected tooth is the only other treatment option. A general practitioner is educated in endodontics and may choose to do some of it in practice. However, when the tooth is difficult to access or has multiple or crooked roots, removing the pulp from it may not be within his/her definition of a great way to spend an afternoon. For these difficult cases referral to an endodontist is usually recommended.

Endodontists thrive on the challenge of removing necrotic tissue to save teeth under conditions that would try the patience of most saints. They may also have to remove a fractured root tip or diseased bone tissue adjacent to the root tip to promote resolution of the infection and encourage growth of healthy new bone. Although clients may find the process of keeping their mouths wide open to provide the best access possible a tiring trial, the endodontist is working even harder on their behalf.

Once the pulp has been removed, the endodontist will use an inert substance to fill the canal and place a temporary restoration in the tooth crown. The family dentist will take over from there and complete the appropriate permanent restoration.

Denturists

Denturists are defined as independent, self-regulated professionals working with other health care practitioners (dentists, dental hygienists, oral surgeons, etc.) to provide oral care. Their scope of practice allows them to provide denture care directly to the public.

In addition to repairing or refitting existing appliances, they can also fit and supply new partial or complete dentures for a client.

In some jurisdictions, denturists can also design and provide dentures which work in conjunction with dental implants.

Part III

How To Survive Dental Treatments

Chapter 6

Hints Your Practitioner Might Not Have Mentioned

In This Chapter

The "during and after" of the following procedures:
- ▶ scaling and root planing
- ▶ application of desensitizing agents
- ▶ topical fluoride application
- ▶ enamel sealant application
- ▶ orthodontic appliance adjustments
- ▶ restoration (filling) placement
- ▶ lasers in restorative dentistry
- ▶ endodontic (root canal) therapy
- ▶ periodontal surgery
- ▶ oral surgery to remove teeth

Scaling and Root Planing

Teeth cleaning appointments are the most commonly performed disease prevention service in dentistry today. Although not usually everyone's favourite process, most people like the tangible results. If you have been harassing your dental plaque on a daily basis with effective tools (see *Chapters 10, 11 and 12*), your regular cleaning appointments (also referred to as recall, recare or preventive maintenance visits) should be fairly easy.

If you have been ducking dental treatment for a while, you may require more extensive care to get back on the path to oral health.

Either way the process is fairly straightforward. Your practitioner, usually a dental hygienist, should:

- ▶ review your health history for changes and consult with the dentist if required

- ▶ note medications taken

- ▶ possibly take your pulse and blood pressure

► perform an extra-oral assessment of lymph glands of the face and the jaw joint for changes or abnormalities

► examine your oral tissues (soft and hard) and note any deviations from normal

► note the amount, location and type of oral deposits present

► take measurements of soft tissue locations if there are signs of periodontal disease

► assess your occlusion

► advise you of the findings and answer any questions you may have

► recommend the dental hygiene interventions appropriate to your needs (oral self-care instruction; removal of deposits; diet analysis and counseling, etc.) and suggest a time frame for their completion

► receive your informed consent to proceed

► carry out the procedures consented to for the remainder of the appointment time

► arrange for the dentist to examine you

► expose and process x-rays if prescribed by the dentist.

If there are minimal deposits (hard calculus or tartar, soft bacterial plaque and superficial stain) on your teeth, the cleaning can usually be completed in one appointment after the examinations are finished. The dental hygienist will use a selection of specially designed powered and hand instruments to remove the plaque and calculus from above and below the gums. The dentist usually does his/her examination once the teeth have been cleaned.

If the dental hygienist's preliminary examination reveals the presence of moderate to heavy deposits and significant soft or hard tissue disease, the dentist is usually called to complete his/her exam early in the appointment. Often x-rays are required so the dentist can make a complete diagnosis and determine which clinical interventions you require. When the x-rays have been assessed you will be advised of steps needed to get your disease under control and teeth restored to function.

The first stage of treatment involves cleaning your mouth and providing information on daily self care. Professional removal of oral deposits and your on-going plaque-control efforts can return your soft tissues to health. If deposits are heavy but soft tissue damage is not extensive, the hygienist will complete the deposit removal. It may take a series of appointments (possibly two to as many as six) to remove accumulated material. Depending on your level of sensitivity, the dentist may administer local anaesthetic in the area before the hygienist proceeds. In some provinces in Canada and some states in the USA, dental hygienists are licensed to administer local anaesthetics. If deposits are heavy and your periodontal disease is moderate to advanced, you may be referred to a periodontist for treatment (see *Chapter 4*).

During deposit removal appointments, expect your hygienist to teach you customized plaque-control measures. At subsequent appointments, your effectiveness in performing these new procedures will be assessed and techniques modified to suit your unique needs.

Instrumentation to remove deposits below the gum line can leave teeth and gums sensitive after scaling appointments. Use warm salt-water rinses two or three times a day for a few days to help reduce the irritation and sensitivity. Place about 2.5 ml (½ tsp) of table salt in a small glass of comfortably warm water. Swish mouthfuls of the water around the tissues for about one minute in total each time you rinse.

Application of Desensitizing Agents

If your gums have receded in some areas of your mouth, the exposed tooth root surfaces can become sensitive to cold, sweets and touch. After your teeth have been cleaned, your hygienist may coat these areas with a special preparation designed to reduce the sensitivity. The area is isolated with cotton rolls, lightly dried and the material applied with a small swab or brush. Saliva is kept off the surface until the material has dried.

There are many formulations of desensitizing agents available for professional application. The most commonly used agents are:

► calcium hydroxide
► sodium fluoride
► sodium silicofluoride
► stannous fluoride
► formalin
► strontium chloride
► zinc chloride-potassium ferrocyanide

The way these products act to reduce sensitivity is not always well understood. It is difficult to obtain good clinical evidence for effectiveness because:

▶ such studies must use subjective reports of effectiveness from the people participating in the study

▶ adequate control for the effect of extraneous variables is not always possible

▶ there is often a strong placebo effect observed among participants assigned to the control group.

After application of desensitizing agents, you may be asked to refrain from rinsing, drinking, eating or smoking for a period of up to four hours in order to give the material the best chance to penetrate the tooth root surface for maximum benefit. For continued results, desensitizing agents may need to be reapplied at subsequent appointments. For some formulations, reduction in sensitivity improves over time with repeated product application.

Desensitizing toothpastes are also available for purchase. If your practitioner advises you to try one of these for added benefit, make sure you are using a product that has Canadian or American Dental Association approval. These toothpastes tend to use five percent potassium nitrate as the active ingredient although other formulations are possible.

Topical Fluoride Application

If you have experienced serious dental decay in the past, your practitioner may want to reduce your risk of future cavity development by applying fluoride to your teeth after they have been cleaned. There are many formulations available for this purpose.

You may be given a rinse to be swished in your mouth for a period of one minute.

Another method of applying fluoride involves isolating your teeth with cotton rolls, drying them and placing trays containing fluoride over them for up to four minutes. Regardless of the type of product used there are some directions you will need to follow:

▶ do **not** swallow the fluoride material

▶ spit out as much of the product as possible when the treatment time is up

▶ do **not** rinse your mouth, eat, drink or smoke for at least one half hour following application to allow maximum penetration of the tooth surface.

Your practitioner may suggest you get daily topical application benefit by using a commercially available home care rinse or toothpaste containing fluoride. Use the products recommended or, if the suggestion is non-specific, select a product that is approved by the Canadian or American Dental Association. Always use any therapeutic product as directed.

For additional information on the use of fluoride in dentistry, see *Chapter 9*.

Enamel Sealant Application

For information on the "what and why" of this procedure, please see *Chapter 10*. Application of these plastic materials to grooves on the biting surfaces of newly erupted teeth (usually permanent ones) is an easy process.

The tooth surfaces to be treated are cleaned and rinsed. The teeth involved are then isolated from mouth fluids using cotton rolls or other simple devices. A weak acid solution is then rubbed on the tooth to prepare the enamel for bonding of the material to it. The acid is then rinsed thoroughly from the tooth and the tooth is dried carefully with compressed air.

The fluid sealant material is painted onto the prepared tooth surface and cured into a solid thin shield. Any extra sealant material is removed and the bite is checked. If the layer of material is too thick it will be reduced until the bite feels normal. There are no post-placement precautions. Sealed teeth function normally and have the benefit of additional protection from decay.

Orthodontic Appliance Adjustments

Once all the fixed orthodontic appliances are in place, teeth are moved by adjustments to the active parts of the system. These consist of arch wires, coil springs and elastics. Adjustment appointments are usually scheduled every four to six weeks until the active phase of treatment is completed and the appliances are removed.

Most appointments involve removal and replacement of the arch wires or coil springs which exert the forces on teeth to create movement. The cellular changes required to move teeth through bone (see *Chapter 3* for details) are similar to the mechanisms of tissue repair in response to injury. For this reason, appliance adjustments create a degree of discomfort for about one to three days. The suggestions below should help you through this period:

▶ eat a soft nutritious diet (milkshakes, eggnog, soups, fruit and vegetable juices, pasta, etc.) to make chewing more comfortable

▶ use salt-water rinses (2.5 ml /½ tsp table salt) in a juice glass of warm water; rinse for a total of one to two minutes several times a day to reduce swelling of tissues

▶ maintain excellent oral hygiene

▶ massage the soft gum tissue gently with a very soft toothbrush or fingertips to increase blood flow in the area which speeds tissue recovery

▶ use over-the-counter analgesics (ASA, ibuprofen, etc.) as directed, if needed

▶ check with your orthodontist if discomfort is intense or prolonged (beyond four days).

Human nature being as it is, when adjustments are made to removable appliances (including head gear and intra-oral elastics) the temptation is to remove the device when the post-operative discomfort sets in. If you yield to this temptation be aware you are only prolonging the ordeal. Each time you remove the appliance you have to start over with the post-operative reaction when you wear it again. This treatment stop-and-start effect is hard on the tissues, increases the period of discomfort and lengthens the whole treatment process. Persevere and wear your removable appliances as directed. In the long run you and your orthodontic treatment team will be happier.

Restoration (Filling) Placement

If your recall intervals are timed according to the effectiveness of your self-care measures, any disease affecting hard tissues should be discovered early. Small decayed areas of teeth will require a simple restoration.

In most instances, restorative treatment will be carried out after administration of local anaesthetic to the area involved. If you tend to be "needle phobic" (or even if you aren't) your practitioner might apply topical anaesthetic ointment to the site prior to making the injection. When this is done, the actual injection can be carried out with minimal or no discomfort.

Once anaesthesia is present, a rubber dam may be placed to keep the operative site dry during the restorative procedure. Use of this device involves placing a snug ring around the back tooth in the area and stretching a sheet of rubber (or vinyl if you have a latex allergy) with holes punched in it over the teeth. Dental floss will carry the rubber dam down through the contacts between the teeth. These actions expose the teeth in the operative site but keep saliva from leaking into the area and also keep water and materials from the operation from sliding into your mouth and down your throat.

Make sure you have asked all of your questions about the procedure before the rubber dam is placed. Conversation becomes very difficult once it is in place.

The dentist will use high-speed instruments to remove the diseased portion of the tooth and design the preparation to receive the restorative material. The most frightening thing about the procedure is the noise of the instruments. For simple restorations, this part of the procedure is relatively short. The most time is taken by placing and contouring the restorative material: the more extensive the damage to the tooth, the more time-consuming the placement and carving of the restoration. For more details about the choices of restorative materials available, please see *Chapter 14*.

Once the filling has been placed and contoured, the rubber dam will be removed and the occlusion (the bite) of the new restoration checked. Some further adjustment may be necessary at this point. If the material used is composite resin, it will have reached its maximum strength during the appointment. If however, amalgam has been used and the filling is complex, you will be cautioned not to chew on that side for the 24-48 hours needed to allow for final set of the material.

The anaesthesia is likely to linger for some time after leaving the office. Take care with the temperature of foods and beverages so you don't burn your mouth. Children are often intrigued by the numb sensation and may be tempted to bite or chew their anaesthetized tongues or lips. Watch them carefully so they do not damage their soft tissue while it is "frozen".

Possible post-operative events include minor soft tissue tenderness at the injection site and possibly from the placement and removal of the rubber dam. The tenderness usually dissipates within a few hours. You may notice some stiffness of the facial muscles, a side effect of keeping your mouth stretched open for a period of time and/or of an injection used to block sensation to one side of the lower jaw. This stiffness usually disappears in 12-24 hours.

Sensitivity to temperature changes may occur in the tooth/teeth restored. Placement of a restoration involves some disturbance to the dentinal tissue which can leave the tooth temporarily sensitive. Protect the tooth from additional trauma by avoiding excessively hot and cold foods and beverages for a few days. Over time, the sensitivity will diminish. If the restoration was close to the pulp, sensitivity may persist for several weeks.

If the sensitivity to cold continues but is diminishing, the tooth is on the road to recovery. **If you notice the restored tooth is becoming increasingly sensitive, particularly to hot foods and beverages, call your dentist for a consultation.** Increasing sensitivity of a tooth to heat is a sign the pulp damage is not resolving and further treatment may be required.

Lasers in Restorative Dentistry

Specially generated light (lasers) have been put to a variety of uses in the last few decades. The best known medical use is probably that of laser eye surgery to correct vision problems.

Lasers are now being used in restorative dentistry. If the decayed area of the tooth is shallow because it has been detected early, laser removal of the damaged tissue may be an option. If laser removal is possible, it can usually be done without the need for administering local anaesthetic. While this is appealing to needle phobics, be aware that laser dentistry may not be coming soon to a dental office near you. Even if it does, not all restorations can be placed using this method. It is also important to remember the best "restoration" is a healthy, undamaged tooth.

Endodontic (Root Canal) Therapy

While no one is likely to volunteer for root canal therapy, the procedure has restored countless teeth to function when the only other option was permanent loss. With modern treatment techniques, facing root canal therapy need not cause excessive anxiety.

When the pulp of a tooth is threatened by encroaching decay it sends out the only sensation its nerves are capable of – pain. If dental treatment is begun before the pulp becomes infected, it may recover and a basic restoration can be placed.

Once infected, the pulp tissue often becomes necrotic, i.e. it's dying, and must be removed to prevent spread of infection throughout the body via the bloodstream. A tooth can function well without its pulp. The only other treatment option for a tooth with an infected pulp is extraction. If factors favour root canal therapy, antibiotics will be prescribed and treatment begun. Depending on the severity of the infection, the process may take one or more appointments. Your family dentist may provide the treatment or choose to refer you to an endodontic specialist.

Usually during single appointment therapy the pulp is removed and the canals filled. Good local anaesthesia should keep you comfortable throughout the appointment. A temporary restoration is placed in the tooth crown to restore function. If the infection has been severe, the pulp may be removed and a bacterial culture taken to determine the effectiveness of the antibiotics. A temporary dressing may be placed in the tooth or it may be left open. Similar cultures will be taken at subsequent appointments until there is no evidence of infection. At that point the canals will be filled and a temporary restoration placed. The temporary filling is left for several weeks to ensure the endodontic therapy has been successful. If the tooth is comfortable and all post-operative events have resolved, your general practitioner will suggest appropriate options for placement of a permanent restoration.

If you have undergone root canal treatment, remember that you started out with an infection and have had subsequent surgery. You may experience some slight facial swelling and possible bruising. If either is severe, seek advice from your practitioner. Some post-operative discomfort is to be expected. Your dentist will likely give you a prescription for analgesics. Take them as directed. If discomfort persists beyond the time frame of your prescribed analgesics, contact your dentist and follow further post-operative management suggestions.

Periodontal Surgery

While no surgical procedure can be described as pleasant, rest assured that with some sensible aftercare, you will benefit from these procedures if they are deemed appropriate. *Chapter 4* describes in some detail the types of periodontal surgical interventions and the rationale for each.

Most periodontal surgeries are accomplished with only local anaesthesia. If you advise your periodontist that you are particularly anxious about the procedure, s/he may prescribe an orally administered anti-anxiety tablet to be taken prior to your appointment. Some practitioners may also use nitrous-oxide sedation during the procedure. If you are anticipating use of either of these calming agents, you should have someone accompany you to the appointment and see you home safely.

At a surgical appointment you may be asked to rinse thoroughly with an oral antiseptic mouthwash prior to the administration of local anaesthesia. These rinses reduce the number of oral bacteria and lower the risk of post-operative infection.

Depending on the procedure, there may be both a tissue donor site and a surgical site in your mouth. According to the practitioner's preference, a dressing may or may not be placed on either or both sites. Periodontal dressings are designed to:

▶   protect the site from trauma

▶   reduce site contamination from oral debris

▶   stabilize the repositioned tissue

▶   assist with wound healing

▶   maintain personal comfort.

The bleeding from both sites will be controlled before you leave the office. Occasionally minor bleeding may recur. If this happens at the tissue donor site, use the gauze sponges you have been given to keep pressure on the area for at least 30 minutes. A damp tea bag can also be used for this purpose. If significant bleeding occurs beyond this time frame, call your practitioner for advice. If the dressing is lost prematurely from the donor site, it usually does not need to be replaced.

If bleeding recurs at the surgical site, call your periodontist and report it. It may mean the flap or graft has been dislodged and professional attention may be required. If the dressing is lost within the first couple of days, report that fact as well. The periodontist may want to check the site and possibly apply a new dressing.

As with all surgery, some post-operative discomfort is to be expected, especially during the first 24 hours following treatment. Your periodontist will probably provide a prescription for analgesic pills. Take them as directed. If pain persists past the time frame estimated by the dentist, call the office for advice and/or renewal of the prescription.

Avoid strenuous exercise for a few days. Eat a normal, well-balanced diet in soft food form. Avoid alcoholic beverages, citrus fruits, and excessively hot, cold or spicy foods.

On the day after surgery, begin oral hygiene practices carefully in the non-surgical areas. Using a small-headed toothbrush may aid oral hygiene as there will be less lip and cheek stretching to accommodate the brush. Less stretching of the facial muscles improves the chances that the dressings will not be prematurely dislodged.

You may have been given a prescription for an antimicrobial (antibacterial) mouthrinse. Use it as directed. These products are designed to lower the bacterial count in the mouth until you are able to perform all manual plaque reduction techniques in all areas as you did prior to surgery. Some of these products may temporarily change your taste perception and leave some superficial stain on tooth surfaces.

You will be scheduled for a post-surgical check five to 10 days following the procedure. At this time, the dressings will be removed and the progress of healing assessed. If everything is satisfactory, the sutures will be taken out (unless absorbable suture products were used) and the areas carefully cleansed of any accumulated debris. If healing is progressing well, the sites will be left uncovered. You should begin gentle oral care in the surgical areas as directed. Full tissue repair may take up to three or four weeks.

Oral Surgery to Remove Teeth

The main aim of today's dental treatment is to keep a full dentition performing at optimal efficiency for its owner for a lifetime. Removal of teeth is considered to be a treatment option of last resort. The main reasons for extraction of teeth are:

► damage to the tooth from traumatic injury or decay beyond the scope of restorative treatment

► removal of selected teeth to alleviate crowding in the arches prior to orthodontic intervention

► removal of impacted teeth to prevent complications which can occur as a result of their presence

► irreversible damage to periodontal tissues such that mobility renders the tooth non-functional.

You may need to have an isolated tooth removed. If this is the case, unless its removal appears to be complicated, the procedure will probably be done by your general practitioner using local anaesthetic. If you need multiple teeth removed, such as four impacted wisdom teeth (third molars) or four premolars for orthodontic purposes, your practitioner may choose to refer you to an oral surgeon.

If the treatment of choice is an immediate full denture placement, please see *Chapter 14* for details of relevant procedures.

For multiple extractions you may be referred to an oral surgeon (for information on their scope of practice, see *Chapter 5*). Oral surgeons offer options regarding pain and anxiety control. Local anaesthesia may be all you feel you require. You will also be offered treatment under a combination of local anaesthesia and various levels of sedation or analgesia (defined as the state in which pain sensation is lost but consciousness is not). Choices are explained in *Chapter 1* under *Options for Pain and Anxiety Control*.

If you have a single extraction site or multiple sites of removal of individual teeth, in each case some aftercare is required. At the time of removal the dentist will have placed a gauze pack over the socket(s) to control the bleeding. It/they should be left in place for at least 30 minutes. Remove it/them carefully so bleeding is not initiated. If bleeding continues, replace the pack(s) with fresh one(s) and keep firm pressure on the area(s) for another 30 minutes. If obvious bleeding is still present, call your dentist for advice.

You may eat soft food and drink warm or cool beverages as soon as the bleeding stops.

Eating very hot or cold foods and beverages can affect stability of the newly formed blood clots. In addition, to maintain the clots and promote healing, you should **not**:

▶ smoke or rinse your mouth for at least 24 hours

▶ use a straw to drink beverages

▶ engage in strenuous activity (e.g. running, lifting heavy weights, etc.) for 24-48 hours.

Control of Swelling and Bruising

Swelling and bruising are typical effects of any type of surgery: the more complex the procedure the more severe the reaction. Although both are part of the normal healing process, measures can be taken to improve comfort levels while they dissipate.

Soft tissue swelling of the face usually peaks 24-48 hours after the surgery. For the first 24 hours, alternate application of cold packs in cycles of 20 minutes on, 20 minutes off will help control the swelling. A refrigerated grain bag (commonly available in health food and naturopathic supply shops) can be applied directly to the swollen face. If you do not have such an item, a bag of frozen peas or crushed ice can be wrapped in a soft towel and used. Do **not** place ice or any other frozen material directly on the skin.

Frequently, ibuprofen is prescribed as a post-operative analgesic. Its anti-inflammatory side effect helps control swelling as well.

By the second post-operative day gentle oral hygiene measures can be performed on the remaining teeth. Use of warm salt-water rinses (2.5 ml or ½ tsp of table salt in a juice glass of warm water) several times a day will assist with oral cleanliness and promote healing. Frequent external application of heat to the facial area will increase blood flow to the site and assist tissue repair.

Bruising is a normal reaction to soft tissue damage. Oral surgery may cause superficial facial bruising. Other than being unsightly, it usually does not indicate a problem and resolves in a few days.

Post-surgical Complications – Alveolitis (Dry Socket)

Normal healing after a tooth extraction involves blood flow into the empty socket where it forms a clot. This clotting mechanism protects the wound and in time is replaced by healthy tissue. Failure of this process can cause the bone in the tooth socket to become inflamed. Dry sockets tend to occur more frequently when mandibular (lower) teeth are extracted. The condition is very painful and onset is usually two to four days after the surgery.

Possible causes of alveolitis include:

► inadequate blood supply to the socket

► infection at the site

► dislodging of the newly formed blood clot by:

  negative oral pressure created by using a straw to drink beverages or by smoking (when drawing on a cigarette, pipe or cigar)

  rinsing the mouth too soon after surgery

  physical trauma from vigorous oral hygiene procedures

  returning too early to a fibrous diet (i.e. one that requires considerable chewing).

Dry socket treatment should be carried out by the dental team. Self-medication will worsen the problem and prolong its resolution. In the office, the affected socket will be:

► irrigated gently with saline solution to remove debris

► packed with iodoform gauze material impregnated with medication to prevent infection and food impaction into the wound and to soothe the nerve endings in the exposed bone.

The dentist may also prescribe antibiotics and/or analgesics to deal with the infection and pain. In-office treatment is repeated every day or two until adequate healing is achieved.

Sensible General Post-surgical Precautions

Avoid the following for at least 24-48 hours:

► smoking

► using a straw to drink beverages

- ▸ rinsing your mouth

- ▸ strenuous exercise (including heavy housework)

- ▸ excessively hot or cold foods and beverages

- ▸ hard, citrus or spicy foods

- ▸ vigorous oral hygiene practices.

To increase comfort and control post-operative effects:

- ▸ use prescribed medications as directed

- ▸ begin careful oral hygiene practices the day after surgery

- ▸ use warm salt-water rinses frequently to reduce swelling and promote healing

- ▸ for facial swelling in the first 24 hours, apply cold packs intermittently (20 minutes on, 20 minutes off). On the second day and after, apply warmth to promote blood circulation.

If you are concerned about any aspect of your post-operative recovery, call your practitioner for assistance.

Part IV

Teeth for a Lifetime

Chapter 7
Dental Anatomy Basics

In This Chapter

- ► basic tooth tissues
- ► types of teeth
- ► two sets of teeth (dentitions)
- ► development of the dentitions
- ► importance of baby teeth
- ► development of occlusion
- ► occlusion in the primary dentition
- ► occlusion in the permanent dentition (Angle's classification)
- ► spacing in the primary dentition
- ► leeway space
- ► other aspects of occlusion (overbite and overjet, crossbites, openbites)

Basic Tooth Tissues

Although teeth come in a variety of types, according to their individual shapes and the chewing function they perform, they all share the same basic anatomical structure. The crown of the tooth is the part which is visible in the mouth. The root portion anchors the tooth in the bony socket.

Each tooth is composed of four tissues. Three of these tissues are mineralized to varying degrees. The pulp at the centre of the tooth is soft and composed of blood vessels, nerves and connective tissue fibres.

To understand dental health it is important to know something about tooth anatomy. Figure 7.1 shows the external parts of a tooth and the internal tissue layers.

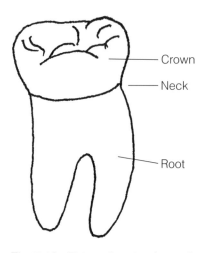

Fig. 7.1A. External parts of a tooth.

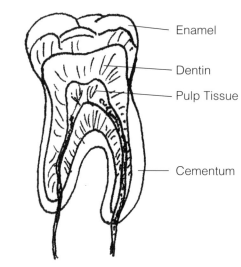

Fig. 7.1B. Internal parts of a tooth.

Types of Teeth

Incisors

In addition to forming the foundation of our smiles, these teeth act as the "scissors" of the dentition, as their name suggests. They are designed as broad, shovel-shaped teeth, with one sharp biting edge.

Fig. 7.2. Example of incisors: a permanent maxillary (upper) central incisor.

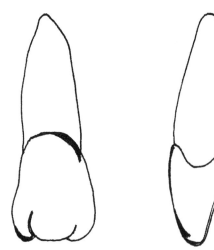

Fig. 7.2C. Biting surface.

Fig. 7.2A. Front.

Fig. 7.2B. Side.

Canines (Cuspids)

These are the pointed teeth (reminiscent of those in dogs) at the corners of the mouth beside the incisors. These "fangs", more prominent in other species of meat eaters, were designed to hold and carry prey. Since humans don't do that, the canines are more subtle in shape. However, they still are heavy, long-rooted teeth with a single point or cusp.

Fig. 7.3. Example of canines (cuspids): a permanent maxillary (upper) cuspid.

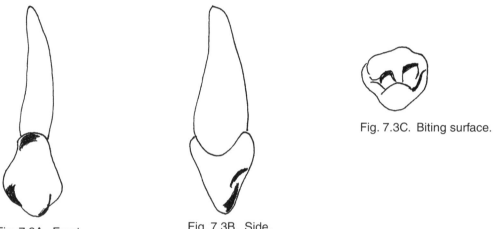

Fig. 7.3C. Biting surface.

Fig. 7.3A. Front.

Fig. 7.3B. Side.

Premolars or Bicuspids

These teeth are named from their form. They have at least two points or cusps (therefore "bi" "cuspid"). Bicuspids can also be described as "mini-molars" or premolars. They function by breaking up larger pieces of food into smaller ones.

Fig. 7.4. Example of premolars (bicuspids): a mandibular (lower) second premolar.

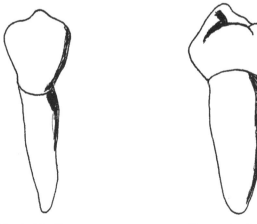

Fig. 7.4C. Biting surface.

Fig. 7.4A. Front.

Fig. 7.4B. Side.

Molars

Molars are the grindstones of the dentition. Their broad surfaces are composed of several rounded cusps which prepare food for swallowing.

Fig. 7.5. Example of maxillary (upper) molars: a permanent first molar.

Fig. 7.5C. Biting surface.

Fig. 7.5A. Front.

Fig. 7.5B. Side.

Fig. 7.6. Example of mandibular (lower) molars: a permanent first molar.

Fig. 7.6C. Biting surface.

Fig. 7.6A. Front.

Fig. 7.6B. Side.

Two Sets of Teeth (Dentitions)

If you are old enough to be reading this book, you already know that humans have two sets of teeth. The first set or primary teeth are often referred to as "baby" teeth. They are adequate while children's faces are small and diets simple. Over time they are replaced with secondary or permanent teeth. This second set is meant to last a lifetime.

Each dentition is made up of a particular number and arrangement of tooth types which were described earlier. The diagrams show the differences between the two sets of teeth.

Fig. 7.7A. Primary dentition: view of the biting surfaces showing arrangement of the various types of teeth in the arches.

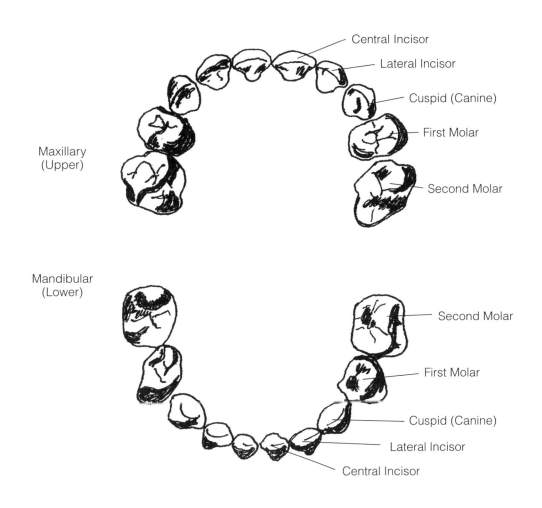

Fig. 7.7B. Primary dentition: side view of half of the dental arches.

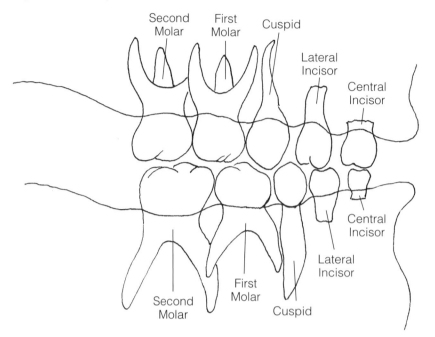

Fig. 7.7C. Permanent dentition: view of the biting surfaces showing arrangement of the various types of teeth in the arches.

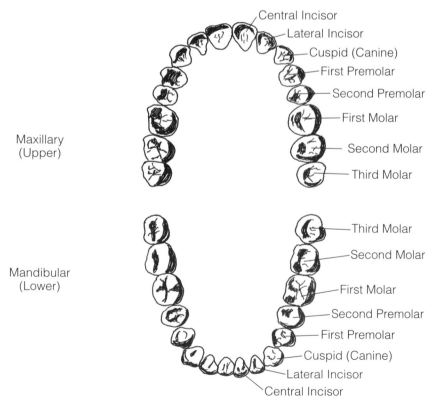

Fig. 7.7D. Permanent dentition: side view of half of the dental arches.

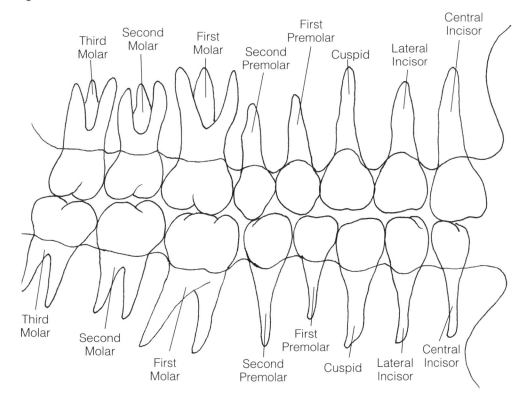

Development of the Dentitions

Dentition is the term used to describe all of the teeth present in the mouth at any given time. In a lifetime, humans have two dentitions. The first 20 years of life are marked by obvious growth and developmental changes in the dentitions. Once all the permanent teeth are in place, the changes are more subtle.

Teeth develop in three major phases:

► calcification and crown completion
► eruption
► root completion

Cells deep in the jawbone carry the genetic information which will create a tooth. This soft tissue begins to incorporate minerals into its mass. This stage of development is known as the first evidence of calcification. Mineralization continues until the finished crown shape of each individual tooth is completed.

Once the crown is mineralized, root formation begins at the base of the crown. As the root material is laid down, the tooth emerges through the gum tissue which covers the bone. This process is called tooth *eruption*. Root development continues after tooth eruption, until the root structure is complete.

Each primary tooth is associated with a group of specialized cells which will create a permanent tooth to replace it. When the internal clock dictates, these cells begin to form the permanent tooth crown. Other cells remove or resorb the root of the primary tooth so that it will be lost to make room for its successor. Dentistry has borrowed terminology from foresters. Normal shedding of primary teeth is called *exfoliation*. Since exfoliation happens to primary teeth, they are also referred to as *deciduous* teeth. Figure 7.8 illustrates the primary teeth in function and the stages of development of the permanent teeth in a child about six to seven years of age.

Fig. 7.8. Primary dentition and permanent tooth development in a child six to seven years of age.

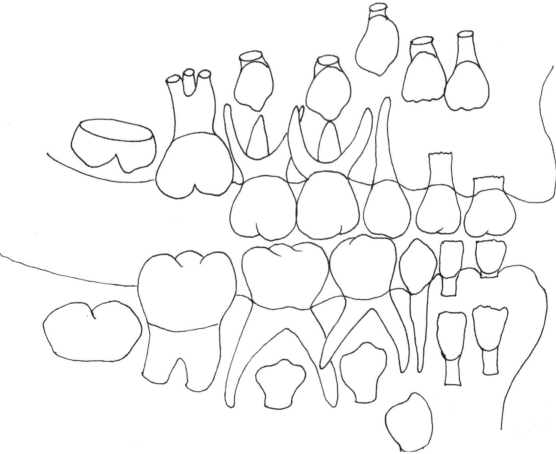

The stages of tooth development occur in an orderly fashion from fetal life through the teen years. The primary dentition develops, emerges and is replaced by the permanent dentition. The timetable of changes for each person is as individual as any characteristic that makes each of us unique. Tooth eruption and replacement are the visible processes of this developmental timetable. Table 7.1 gives you an idea of the average time frame or chronology of development of the primary dentition and table 7.2 the average timing of appearances of the permanent teeth.

Remember that there can be variations in the timing of events in growth and development which are perfectly normal. However, if you notice large differences between what to expect and what is happening, you should seek advice from your dental professional.

Table 7.1 Chronology of the Primary Dentition	
Tooth Type	Age of Eruption in Months
central incisors	8-12
lateral incisors	9-13
first molars	13-19
canines (cuspids)	16-22
second molars	25-33

Table 7.2 Chronology of the Permanent Dentition		
Age of Eruption in Years Upper (Maxillary) Teeth	Tooth Type	Age of Eruption in Years Lower (Mandibular) Teeth
7-8	central incisors	6-7
8-9	lateral incisors	7-8
11-12	canines (cuspids)	9-10
10-11	first premolars	10-12
10-12	second premolars	11-12
6-7	first molars	6-7
12-13	second molars	11-13
17-22	third molars	17-22

Importance of Baby Teeth

Baby's first tooth is a milestone in the development of a child that delights parents. It is a sign of normal growth and development of the infant. Soon that one tooth is followed by others. As they increase in number, mom knows that the end of providing separate meals for baby is approaching.

Teething is usually accompanied by a desire to chew, excessive drooling or appetite changes and sometimes signs of fever in the child. If babies experience discomfort during teething, they usually let parents know in the only way they have to express themselves: they cry. If this happens in the wee hours of the morning, parents can become less than enchanted by the teething process. For tips on dealing with teething infants, to help both baby and parents through the process, see information at the end of this chapter.

Too often the appearance of children's teeth, heralded as a cause of celebration, can turn into a cause for consternation if they decay. When faced with dental bills parents' attitudes often change to "They're only baby teeth. Why bother repairing them?" There are four important reasons for maintaining a healthy primary dentition. They are:

▶ to enable the growing child to eat a proper diet which influences the development of a balanced face

▶ to guide the permanent teeth into appropriate positions

▶ to assist in the development of correct speech

▶ to maintain a pleasing appearance.

Nutrition and Facial Balance

As the infant grows, a "milk only" diet is no longer sufficient for adequate nutrition. Babies gradually need to be introduced to a wide variety of foods with essential nutrients required for growth and health.

A balanced diet includes foods with differing textures. Here is where the facial balance aspect comes in. As facial muscles add chewing function to the already well developed sucking habits, the dynamics of facial bone growth are changed.

Bones of the face develop in harmony with facial muscles under function. Healthy teeth, distributed normally along the dental arches, and chewing crisp textured foods are essential to the development of balanced facial muscles. Balanced facial muscles, in turn, contribute to symmetrical development of the underlying facial bones.

Primary Teeth as "Path Finders"

Each primary tooth in the dentition starts to form before birth. During fetal development and in the first few months after birth the crown of the tooth continues to form. Once the crown is completed, the teeth emerge into the mouth as described earlier. Each primary tooth has a group of cells associated with it which will, in time, create the permanent tooth which will replace it.

It is important that the primary tooth remain healthy and in place until the crown of its permanent successor is completed. If the primary tooth loses its dimension due to damage or decay, or worse yet, if it is lost entirely, space can be lost in the dental arch which is needed to accommodate the larger secondary tooth. When arch length is lost, erupting permanent teeth will often change their path of development and emerge in the mouth out of proper position.

Speech Development

Humans have the most highly developed vocalization patterns in the animal kingdom. It is that capacity to use complex spoken language which truly sets humans apart from other animals. The production of spoken words is an immensely complex mental and physiological process.

In a gross simplification of the process, speech is produced when the brain, nerves and muscles co-ordinate to force air from the lungs over the vocal cords and through the mouth. Sounds are produced and modified using: lips, cheeks, tongue and last, but not least, teeth.

The drive to acquire language as a form of communication is innate. All infants begin life with the ability to make vocal noises to summon adults to appropriate action to satisfy their needs. In addition, babies babble and coo, seemingly randomly. With increasing age, these random sounds become more imitative of the language children hear and they begin to organize the sounds into meaningful syllables and words.

Language develops over the first two to three years of life – the same time frame as the eruption of primary teeth. Tooth malposition or loss can impair the development of normal speech patterns.

Teeth and Attractiveness

While it may be true that "beauty is only skin deep" there is no question that what the bodily package looks like has a profound impact on how other people react. A child with obviously diseased or missing teeth can be rejected or ridiculed by peers. Even adults may, without realizing it, treat children with oral problems differently. How many Halloween witches are portrayed with radiant smiles?

Tooth and gum diseases are often accompanied by halitosis (bad breath). Mouth malodour discourages others from close interaction with the individual who has it.

Teething Tips for Baby and Parents

During the teething process, babies will have a natural tendency to chew whatever is at hand. The objective is to encourage the emerging teeth through the gum tissue, not a sign that the child is necessarily hungry. They will chew fingers, toes, blankets, toys or adults' fingers. The most desirable objects are often those that are firm and cool. Baby departments of grocery stores and pharmacies offer a wide range of teething objects and medicaments.

Since chewing during the teething stage does not imply hunger, "teething biscuits" should not be presented except as an accompaniment for meals. Most of these foods have enough sugar content to be damaging to the teeth already present if they are used frequently to comfort the child.

Plastic or rubber teething devices are available which satisfy the child's need to chew without posing a risk of tooth decay. These come in a variety of shapes. Ensure that they are not small enough to be swallowed and are sturdy enough that the child cannot bite off and swallow pieces of the material. Some of them are fluid filled and can be cooled in the refrigerator or freezer. Follow the manufacturer's instruction regarding care and use of these products.

Over-the-counter medication is available for application to the child's gums to relieve discomfort. Use these products only if other measures are not adequate and always as directed. If your child runs a fever while teething, check with your dentist or pediatrician to see if a child's dose of aspirin is indicated.

Teething Checklist for the Child's Relief

▶   Keep a supply of clean, cool, firm objects available for the child to chew on.

▶   Ensure that teething devices are intact and large enough that they cannot be swallowed.

▶   Wash the teething devices frequently in hot water and dish detergent.

▶   Present "teething biscuits" only as part of a meal.

► If the child is persistently uncomfortable in spite of the actions listed above, consider use of a topically applied medication **used only as directed**.

► Consult with a dentist or pediatrician regarding use of fever-reducing medication if indicated.

Teething Checklist for Adult Relief

► Teething is easier to cope with (even at two o'clock in the morning) by remembering that it is a stage, like many others, through which the child will pass and usually the family will emerge unscathed.

Development of Occlusion

Before information on the treatment of malocclusions is presented, it is useful to understand how occlusion develops. Since treatment options are dependent on the type of malocclusion that needs to be corrected, the major classification systems will be discussed. (For further discussion of occlusion and malocculsion, see *Chapter 3*.)

There are three major phases to the development of occlusion. The first phase occurs when only primary or baby teeth are in function. Over time, primary teeth are replaced with permanent ones. During this transition phase both primary and permanent teeth are present in the mouth. This second stage of dental development is referred to as the *mixed dentition* phase. The third and final phase occurs when all primary teeth have been replaced and only permanent teeth make up the dentition.

Development of occlusion is a dynamic process. There are four major physiological factors involved. Each of the following will be described in turn:

► occlusion in the primary and permanent dentitions

► spacing patterns of teeth in the primary dentition

► size differences between primary teeth and their permanent replacements (leeway space)

► mesial drift.

Occlusion in the Primary Dentition

Classification of occlusion in the primary dentition is referred to as Terminal Plane Relationship. The "terminal planes" involved are the distal (backward facing) surfaces of the primary second molars. How these surfaces line up from the tooth in the upper jaw to the one in the lower arch with which it bites determines the relationship designation. The diagrams in this section illustrate the three possible relationships.

Straight or Flush Terminal Plane

As you can see, the distal surfaces of the key teeth are in line, one directly above the other. About 80 percent of children have this classification with their baby teeth.

Fig. 7.9A. Straight or Flush Terminal Plane occlusion in the primary dentition.

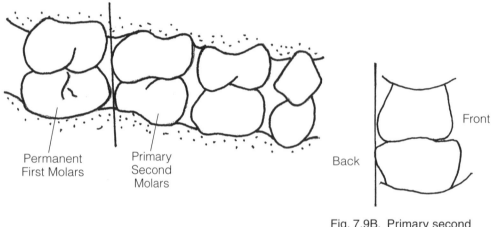

Permanent
First Molars

Primary
Second
Molars

Back   Front

Fig. 7.9B. Primary second
molar relationship.

Mesial Step Terminal Plane

This class gets its name from the fact that the lower second molar is positioned more towards the front of the mouth (more mesial) than its upper antagonist. To draw a line to determine the relationship you must move down and towards the front of the mouth. The resulting line looks rather like a stair step towards the mesial.

This class accounts for about 15 percent of primary occlusions.

Fig. 7.10A. Mesial Step occlusion in the primary dentition.

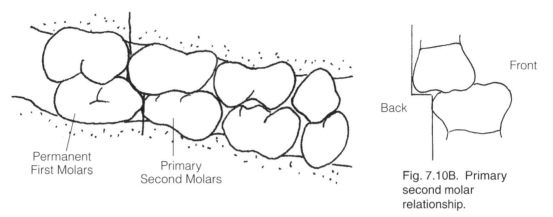

Permanent
First Molars

Primary
Second Molars

Fig. 7.10B. Primary
second molar
relationship.

Front

Back

Distal Step Terminal Plane

This third possibility is the opposite of the Mesial Step Terminal Plane. The second primary molar in the upper arch is forward in the mouth relative to the opposing tooth in the lower arch. To draw a line to determine the relationship you must move down and towards the back of the mouth or towards the distal. Again the line looks like a stair step in the distal direction.

A relatively small percentage of children display this relationship. However, when it occurs, it is usually a strong sign that a facial growth problem is present. Children with this growth pattern should be observed carefully so that necessary orthodontic intervention can be timed optimally.

Fig. 7.11A. Distal Step occlusion in the primary dentition.

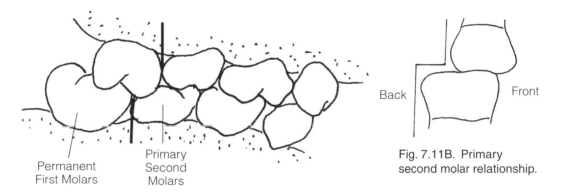

Permanent
First Molars

Primary
Second
Molars

Back

Front

Fig. 7.11B. Primary
second molar relationship.

Occlusion in the Permanent Dentition (Angle's classification)

The most commonly used classification system is that devised by Dr. Charles H. Angle. He gave his name to the system. The somewhat geometrical reference is purely coincidental.

Angle's classification uses specific permanent teeth to define the front-to-back or anterior-posterior relationships of the jaws. The teeth identified to do this are; the permanent first molars, canines and central incisors. From observation, Angle discovered that the first permanent molars were important to development of satisfactory occlusion in the adult. He further determined reference points on the molars to describe relationships between them.

Since Angle was observing adult dentitions in an era when preventive dentistry was almost unknown, many of the people he saw were missing first molars. He discovered that the classes of occlusion could be determined from the canine teeth (usually highly resistant to loss from either accident or decay) and by the central incisors.

Angle's Class I

In this class, the *mesiobuccal* (outer front) cusp of the upper first permanent molar is in line with the *mesiobuccal groove* of the lower first permanent molar. This places the lower molar slightly forward of the upper and should remind you of the Mesial Step Terminal Plane (MSTP) relationship in the primary dentition described earlier in the chapter. With well-aligned arches this creates a canine relationship where the upper tooth is just back of (or distal to) the lower canine.

Angle considered Class I relationships ideal to proper functioning. Class I occlusion occurs when the teeth are well-aligned with adequate space. If the molars and canines displayed the proper relationship but teeth were crowded, tipped or rotated, Angle called the pattern Class I *malocclusion*. Class I is still the most common form of malocclusion.

Fig. 7.12A. Angle's Class I occlusion in the permanent dentition.

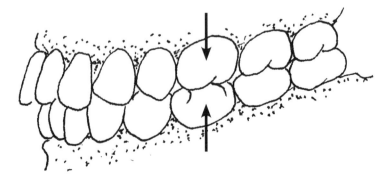

Fig. 7.12C. Class I cuspid relationship.   Fig. 7.12B. Class I first molar relationship.

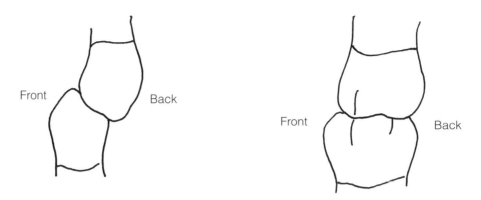

Front   Back   Front   Back

All of the remaining possibilities for relationships among the key teeth constitute malocclusions as they all deviate from what Angle considered was ideal.

Angle's Class III

Since this is an easier class to discuss it will be dealt with now and Class II will follow. Class III occlusion can be thought of as an exaggerated Class I. The lower arch is forward relative to the upper arch. When pronounced, you can recognize this facial pattern in people who have protruding lower jaws.

Fig. 7.13A. Angle's Class III malocclusion in the permanent dentition.

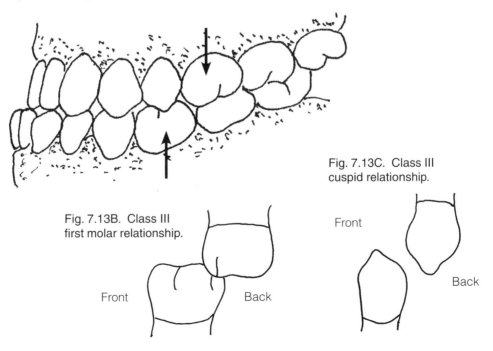

Fig. 7.13C. Class III cuspid relationship.

Fig. 7.13B. Class III first molar relationship.

Front   Back

Front

Back

Angle's Class II

Hold on, this is where things become trickier. The final possibility for front-to-back relationship of the molars is shown in figure 7.14.

As you can see, the upper molar is forward of the lower tooth reminiscent of the Distal Step Terminal Plane (DSTP) in the primary dentition described earlier in the chapter. In fact, a Distal Step will guide the permanent molars into a Class II relationship. This malocclusion is almost always accompanied by a facial growth imbalance.

Fig. 7.14A. Angle's Class II malocclusion in the permanent dentition.

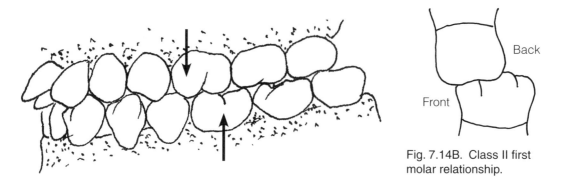

Back

Front

Fig. 7.14B. Class II first molar relationship.

The two possibilities for the placement of the canine teeth in Angle's Class II malocclusion depend on the degree of displacement of the molars. Figure 7.15 shows these possibilities.

Fig. 7.15. Class II cuspid relationship (two possibilities).

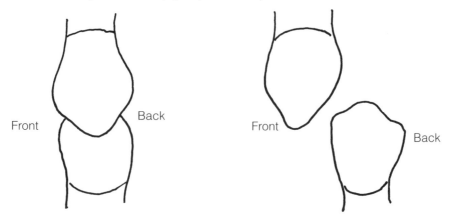

Front   Back

Front   Back

Angle also observed two common patterns of incisor placement to accompany Class II molar and canine relationships. He used these patterns to determine two sub-categories to Class II malocclusions which he named Divisions 1 and 2. The central incisor relationships which determine these divisions are shown in figure 7.16.

Fig. 7.16. Class II permanent central incisor relationships, Division 1 (left) and Division 2 (right).

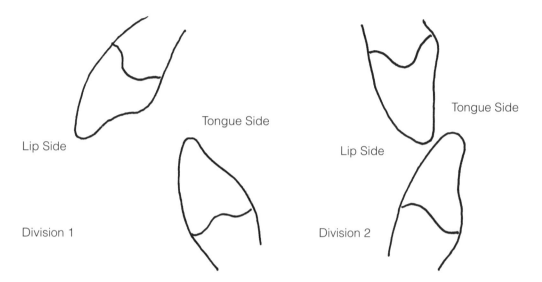

In Division 1, the front teeth slant towards the lips. You can easily recognize this as a person with "buck" teeth. Since this problem is so easily identified on casual observation, it is the malocclusion most frequently treated by orthodontists even though it is not the most common.

In Division 2, the front teeth tend to slant slightly towards the tongue. Often the front teeth are otherwise well-aligned making the face and smile look quite normal. Sometimes, the upper front teeth are crowded or the lateral incisors (the teeth second from the midline of the mouth) stick out towards the lips making the problem more obvious. Either way, Division 2 malocclusions tend to be under-recognized, both by parents and professionals, and often go untreated.

If this is making sense to you, you may already be realizing that Mesial Step occlusion in the primary dentition will lead to Class I molar relationship in the permanent teeth. You are absolutely right. Remember, only about 15 percent of children have Mesial Step occlusion. So what happens for the rest of the majority who develop Class I molar relationships? Some additional information is required to answer that question. Factors involved are:

▶ spacing patterns in the primary dentition

▶ size differences between certain primary teeth and the permanent teeth that replace them (leeway space)

▶ a phenomenon known as mesial drift.

Spacing in the Primary Dentition

Adult teeth typically contact their neighbours on either side in the same arch. This is not true of most primary teeth. Baby teeth tend to be distributed along the arch with distinct patterns of space occurring between them. This is good news since the permanent teeth that will eventually replace them are considerably larger. Although the face grows as the baby teeth are replaced by permanent ones, extra space between the baby teeth in the arch is a hedge against crowding of the adult teeth. Each of these spacing possibilities will be discussed in turn.

Generalized Spacing

In this pattern, the canines and molars tend to contact one another. The front teeth tend to have spaces between them.

Fig. 7.17. Generalized spacing in the primary dentition.

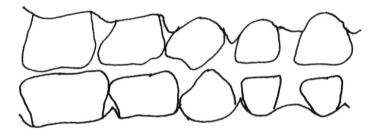

Primate Spacing

This pattern is one that is observed in other primate animals (apes, chimpanzees, etc.) as well as in humans. The baby teeth tend to be in contact except for exaggerated spaces between the upper lateral incisor and canine and between the lower canine and first molar.

Fig. 7.18. Primate spacing in the primary dentition.

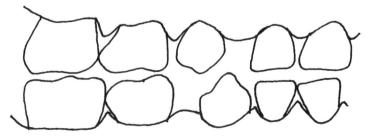

Combination Spacing

As the name suggests, this pattern is a combination of the two patterns already described. It has the generalized spacing of the front teeth and the exaggerated spaces of the primate pattern rolled into a single dentition. Few children displaying this pattern will suffer from crowding problems with their permanent teeth.

Fig. 7.19. Combination spacing in the primary dentition.

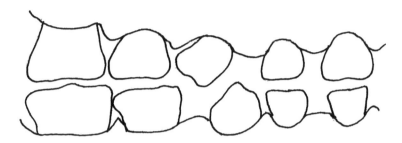

Closed Primary Dentition

Although often favoured by parents and advertisers as the most pleasing in appearance, this pattern usually foretells of crowding problems. A closed primary dentition mirrors that of the adult, with teeth in contact with neighbours throughout the arches. With no extra space available, this pattern almost guarantees that the larger permanent teeth will need assistance to find adequate room for proper alignment.

Fig. 7.20. Closed primary dentition.

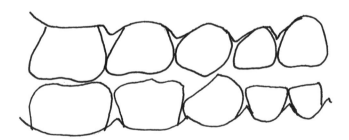

Leeway Space

A quick look at the teeth of a four-year-old and an adult is enough to determine that baby teeth are much smaller than permanent ones. However, in order to understand a bit more about the development of occlusion during the transition phase from one dentition to the next, a more careful examination of the size differences is important.

The teeth that require consideration are the:

▶ canines, both primary and permanent

▶ the baby molars

▶ the permanent premolars that replace the primary molars.

If front-to-back (mesiodistal) measurements are made of each tooth listed above, you will note that the combined arch length used by the baby canines and molars is longer than that required for the permanent canines and premolars. The "leftover" space occurring when permanent teeth replace the primary ones is called "leeway". Figure 7.21 shows this relationship.

Fig. 7.21. Leeway space.

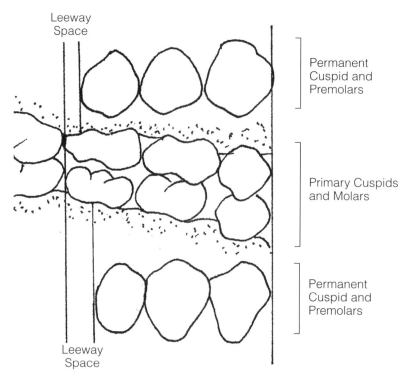

Fortuitously, there is more space available in the lower arch than in the upper. This leeway space on its own or in combination with other spacing patterns in the primary dentition facilitates development of an Angle's Class I molar relationship from Straight Terminal Plane occlusion of the baby teeth.

Straight or Flush Terminal Plane occlusion of the primary molars (which, you will remember, occurs in the majority of cases) leads to an early Angle's Class II molar relationship of the permanent first molars. However, if the baby molars are lost naturally, the permanent molars will move forward in a normal phenomenon known as *mesial drift*. With extra space available in the lower arch, the permanent molars have a good chance to establish a sound Class I relationship through what is often called a "mesial shift".

Other Aspects of Occlusion (Overbite and Overjet, Crossbites, Openbites)

Overbite and Overjet

Analysis of occlusion must also take into consideration the vertical relationship of teeth in the arches in addition to their front-to-back relationship. When teeth are in occlusion, the upper teeth normally overlap the bottom teeth. The degree of overlap is termed *overbite* and is measured using the central incisors. Overbite is measured in two planes: vertical and horizontal. Horizontal overbite can also be called *overjet*. Figure 7.22 illustrates overbite relationships.

Fig. 7.22. Overbite and overjet.

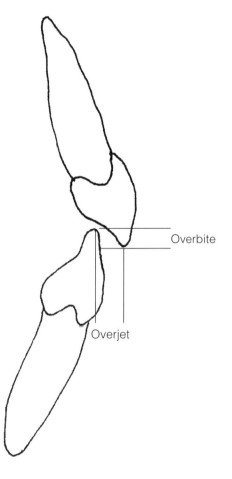

Crossbites

Since the front teeth have a single cutting edge, this means that the upper teeth can be seen to hide part of the lower teeth. The back teeth that have broader chewing surfaces occlude with the upper teeth overlapping the lowers by half of their cheek-to-tongue dimensions. Any deviation from this overlapping arrangement is called a *crossbite*.

Crossbites can occur anywhere in the arch. A crossbite may involve only two teeth or several. Figure 7.23 illustrates some commonly seen crossbite possibilities.

Fig. 7.23A. Examples of anterior crossbites.

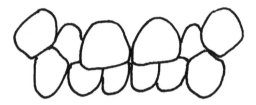

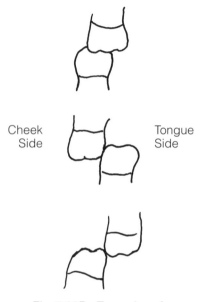

Cheek Side　　　Tongue Side

Fig. 7.23B. Examples of posterior crossbites.

Openbites

When some individuals bite on their back teeth, other teeth in the arch may not overlap at all. This situation is called *openbite*. An openbite may occur anyplace along the arch and involve two or more teeth. One common occurrence of openbite is the result of an abnormal swallowing pattern or tongue thrust. An example of a commonly seen openbite is shown in figure 7.24.

Fig. 7.24. Example of an openbite.

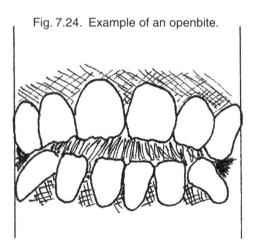

Chapter 8
Mouth Problems

In This Chapter

- ▶ prevalence of oral disease
- ▶ two types of oral disease
- ▶ the B-S-T of tooth decay
- ▶ severe tooth decay in infants (infant caries syndrome)
- ▶ periodontal disease
- ▶ top 10 "plaque facts"
- ▶ self checks for oral cancer

Prevalence of Oral Disease

Diseases of the mouth or oral cavity have plagued humankind since the dawn of civilization. Earliest identified human remains show evidence of oral disease. Many strategies to combat these diseases have been practised over thousands of years of human history. In spite of all efforts they still persist. Other parts of this book explain the current arsenal of defensive weapons.

Who suffers from these diseases? Oral disease of one type or another affects everyone to some degree at some stage of the life cycle. It is the truly universal aspect of human beings. Oral disease knows no linguistic, geographic, cultural, gender or age boundaries. It is an equal-opportunity infection. Anyone with a mouth is susceptible.

Two Types of Oral Disease

Oral diseases are divided into two basic types. The more familiar is tooth decay (or in the jargon of the dental professional – *dental caries*). As the name implies, this disease attacks only the teeth. Tooth decay progresses slowly and is initially painless. If unchecked, it can lead to intense pain (as anyone who has ever suffered from a toothache can attest). Eventually it causes disfiguration, loss of function and finally loss of the tooth involved.

The second type of oral disease infects the supporting structures in the mouth. Untreated it will ultimately destroy the gums and bone which anchor teeth. Many people are unaware that periodontal disease, as it is called, accounts for loss of more teeth than does tooth decay! Figure 8.1 shows the anatomy of these periodontal (meaning around + tooth) tissues when they are healthy.

Fig. 8.1. Healthy tooth and periodontal tissues.

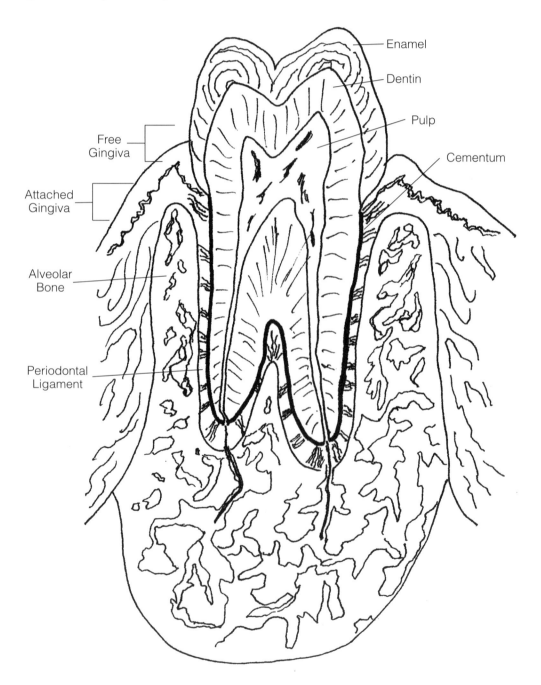

The tendency is to associate tooth decay with children and consider periodontal disease an inevitable part of aging. It is important to remember both of these diseases can be harmful at any age. Understand too that tooth loss is not a "normal part of aging".

The actual causes of tooth decay and periodontal disease became well understood only during the last half of the 20th century. Throughout most of history, dentistry has concentrated on repairing the ravages of disease. Experience indicates that the finest restoration is a poor substitute for healthy oral tissues.

Knowing the causes of oral disease increases the ability to treat it. Better yet, this knowledge fosters ways of preventing it. Health promotion strategies are covered in other chapters.

The B-S-T of Tooth Decay

With the development of scientific knowledge, the "whys" of any observed phenomenon generate very interesting theories as explanations. The theories around the process of tooth decay are no exception.

It is now known tooth decay involves the following factors:

▶ bacteria

▶ sugar or starches

▶ teeth

The process is dynamic. Bacteria of various kinds live in the mouth constantly. In controlled numbers and in an unorganized state they do little harm. As living organisms they do what all living things do: they eat, excrete and multiply. Although not social beings in a sophisticated sense, they do prefer to organize into colonies known as *plaque* or *biofilm*. Once organized, plaque sticks to tooth surfaces in areas of the mouth where it is least likely to be disturbed.

As living organisms, bacteria need food to survive. Their favourite foods are sugars and starches, also popular choices of many people. Bacteria discharge waste products of metabolism in the form of acids. When plaque forms, the large numbers of bacteria in it produce enough acid to be dangerous to teeth.

The structure of plaque holds the acid waste close to the tooth surface and slows down the rate at which saliva can penetrate the mass to neutralize it. Over time, with repeated acid attacks, the mineralized tooth tissues dissolve.

Once the hard enamel covering of the tooth has been penetrated, the softer layers decay more quickly. Figure 8.2 illustrates the progress of tooth decay. While the mineralized layers of the teeth decay, there is usually little or no discomfort. Once the disease gets close to the pulp, the tooth may become very painful. At this stage, bacteria can access other parts of the body via the bloodstream. This can cause symptoms of systemic illness such as aches and fever.

For individuals with lowered immune system function, synthetic joints or heart valves, infection from oral diseases can be very dangerous, in fact, life-threatening.

Fig. 8.2 Process of tooth decay.

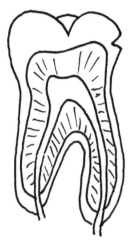

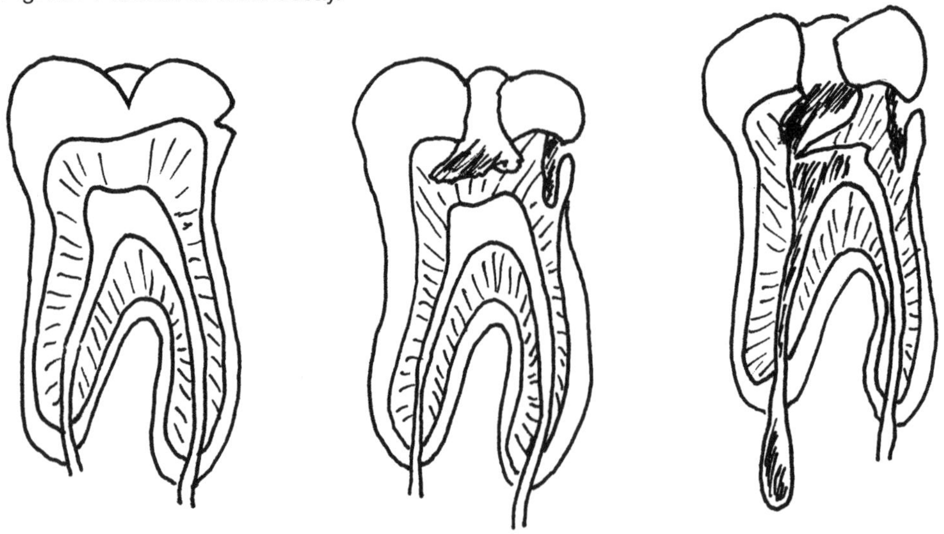

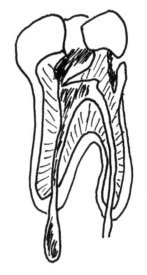

Fig. 8.2A. Defects affect enamel tissue.

Fig. 8.2B. Decay spreads more rapidly when reaching dentin.

Fig. 8.2C. When decay reaches the pulp tissue, infection can cause an abscess and spread through the bloodstream.

Severe Tooth Decay in Infants (Infant Caries Syndrome)

Tooth decay can be devastating at any age. Probably the most disheartening form is its occurrence in infants and preschool children. Children's teeth begin to emerge into the mouth at about six months of age. As soon as that happens they become vulnerable to decay. As long as bacterial plaque is allowed to accumulate on them and sugar is eaten frequently, decay will happen.

Sources of Sugar

► breast milk

► infant formula

► fruit juices (unsweetened juice contains natural fruit sugars and sweetened juice has added refined sugar)

▸ "natural" sugars such as honey, corn syrup, maple syrup, etc., used on soothers or pacifiers to calm a cranky child.

The Time Factor

▸ Unlimited access to the breast or a bottle of liquid containing sugar: teeth of children who nurse many times a day are exposed to additional acid attacks which can cause decay.

▸ Allowing the infant to fall asleep during nursing either at the breast or with a bottle: during sleep, two things occur which increase the child's risk of tooth decay. First, the sweet liquid tends to pool in the child's mouth which increases the plaque's supply of nutrients. Secondly, the flow of saliva diminishes, causing plaque acids to be neutralized more slowly. Acid therefore has more time to do damage.

▸ Frequent use of pacifiers dipped in sugars of any kind.

▸ Persistent use of a bottle or "sippy cup" filled with milk or juice for toddlers (two years and up). These children are well past the age of being able to drink from a cup and should be encouraged to do so when thirsty. Sipping sugary liquids over prolonged periods of the day increases the risk of tooth decay significantly. If the child is thirsty between meals, offer water. It is a better thirst quencher and body hydrator than a sweet drink.

Tooth decay can occur rapidly in children, given the appropriate risk factors. Children's teeth are tiny. Compared to their overall size, there is less mineralized tissue covering the soft inner pulp. When exposed to plaque acids, decay can progress to serious stages more rapidly than in an adult tooth. If decay is allowed to progress, it can become very severe. Serious decay of primary teeth is called *nursing caries* or *infant caries syndrome*. Figure 8.3 shows the progression of this type of tooth decay.

Fig. 8.3. Infant caries syndrome: pattern of tooth decay in infants.

Fig. 8.3A. Early stage.   Fig. 8.3B. Late stage.

Fortunately infant tooth decay is almost entirely preventable by following the few simple rules outlined in *Chapter 11*.

Periodontal Disease

"Periodontal" means "around the tooth". It is an adjective used to describe tissues which surround and support the teeth. These tissues include:

▶ Specialized skin tissue in the gums or *gingiva* (where "g" is pronounced as in ginger)

▶ The *periodontal ligament*: a band of fibres (made up of specialized cells known as connective tissue) which holds the tooth in its bony socket

▶ *Alveolar bone* (the spongy bone which surrounds tooth roots).

The relationship of these tissues to one another and to the tooth they support is illustrated in figure 8.4.

Fig. 8.4A. Periodontal tissues.

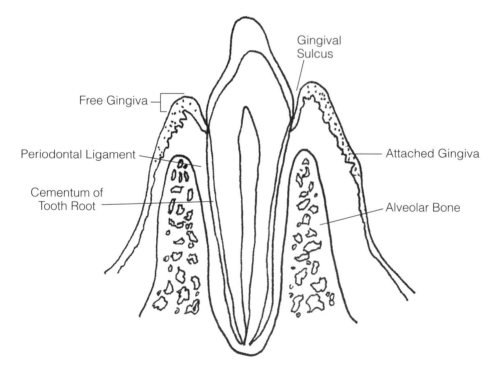

Fig. 8.4B. A closer view.

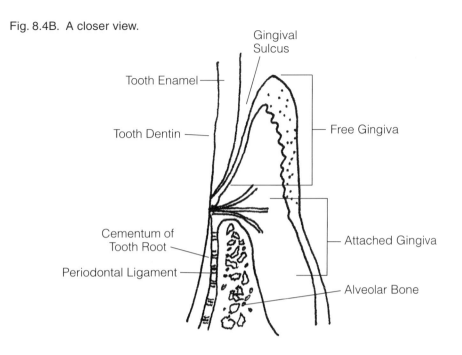

As indicated earlier in this chapter, periodontal disease causes loss of more teeth than does decay. The disease process in periodontal tissues is also more complicated.

While some types of bacteria in plaque produce acids which dissolve teeth, others generate waste products which affect the gums and bone. Bacterial plaque grows best where it is protected from disturbance either from chewing activities or brushing techniques. This means heaviest accumulation occurs between teeth, along the gum line and under the gums at the necks of teeth.

Mature bacterial plaque will incorporate minerals from saliva or the adjacent tooth into the mass. This creates a hard substance commonly called "tartar" and scientifically known as *calculus*. This hard deposit provides increased surface area for plaque growth. Calculus removal from above and below the gum line is a job for professionals.

Periodontal diseases are classified according to the type of tissue affected. Disease which attacks only the soft skin tissue is called *gingivitis*. Disease which destroys connective tissue and bone is referred to as *periodontitis*.

Gingivitis – A Reversible Invasion

Just as in the process of tooth decay, huge numbers of bacteria organize into plaque and generate enough toxic waste to cause inflammation and infection of the periodontal tissues. The first reaction to the assault is in the gum tissue.

Normal gingiva is firm, "knife-edged" at the borders and closely contoured to the necks of the teeth. It is stippled in texture, like an orange peel. Colour varies according to race and may be coral pink or mottled with brown or dark purple pigmentation.

When attacked by plaque wastes, several changes occur. The gingiva becomes enlarged and it no longer fits snugly around the tooth neck. As it swells it loses firmness and stippling. In tissues without pigmentation, the colour changes from coral pink to red or bluish-red. Colour changes in pigmented tissues are more subtle and harder to recognize.

As these changes occur, the gingiva becomes fragile and will bleed easily under minor stress. Usually this is first noticeable when you brush your teeth. As gingival health declines, the tissues may bleed when you eat or touch them with your finger. This is referred to as "spontaneous bleeding".

Most people would be upset if their fingers or toes bled when touched or when performing their normal function. Surprisingly, many people can observe their bleeding gums without concern. Bleeding anywhere in the body is an indication the skin covering is no longer intact. Among other things, skin is designed to keep blood and body fluids in and bacteria out. Loss of skin integrity anywhere on the body increases the risk of illnesses due to bacterial invasion.

Dental professionals can recognize all gingival changes. This is one good reason for having regular oral examinations. Non-professionals who don't recognize subtle changes can use the presence of gingival bleeding as a barometer of gingival tissue health. If your gums bleed, you should be concerned and have the cause investigated. Early professional assistance can prevent more serious damage.

When gingival disease is caught early, tissues can be returned to health, usually without permanent damage. The first step in professional treatment is to remove the source of the inflammation. Once this is done you may be coached to adopt new home care habits to maintain health. This topic is covered thoroughly in *Part V* of this book.

Periodontitis – A Permanent Change

When the gums become inflamed and fragile, they no longer hug the necks of the teeth like a snug turtleneck sweater. Flabby gums allow more bacterial plaque to accumulate, mature and mineralize. Once calculus (tartar) is formed it increases the surface area for plaque development. Calculus protects plaque from being disturbed by most home oral cleaning techniques. With the development of plaque-covered calculus above and below the gum line, the conditions are right for the spread of infection to deeper periodontal tissues.

The fibres that make up the periodontal ligament are attached at one end to the *cementum* (specialized tissue which covers the surface of the tooth root) and at the other to the alveolar bone which forms the tooth socket. This ligament acts as a shock absorber during chewing to prevent fracture of the teeth and/or bone under heavy biting forces.

Alveolar bone exists solely as a support for teeth. When teeth are lost, the body removes the adjacent alveolar bone. While teeth are present, the bone is constantly being remodeled in response to stimuli transmitted through the periodontal ligament.

Bacterial invasion can destroy the periodontal ligament and alveolar bone. Treatment interventions can halt destruction and return health to the remaining tissue mass. Once lost, however, it is nearly impossible to regenerate either periodontal ligament fibres or alveolar bone. The damage done by periodontitis is considered to be irreversible. Figure 8.5 illustrates the progression of periodontal disease.

Fig. 8.5 Progress of periodontal disease.

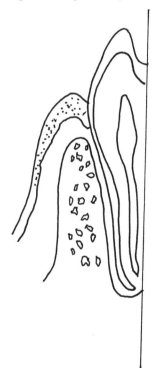 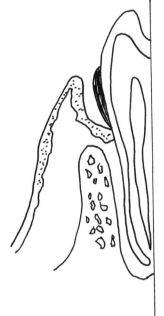 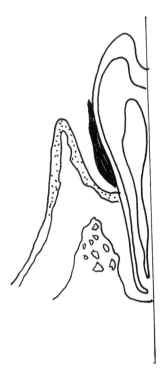

Fig. 8.5A. Healthy tissue. Fig. 8.5B. Gingival inflammation. Fig. 8.5C. Pocket formation and bone loss.

Top 10 "Plaque Facts"

► Many different species of bacteria live in the mouth.

► Some species generate acidic waste products which decay teeth.

► Other species attack supporting tissues of the teeth (periodontal tissues).

► Oral bacteria constantly attempt to organize into established colonies called plaque.

► It takes bacteria approximately 24 hours to establish plaque structure at a level which will initiate disease.

► Plaque formation occurs where potential disturbance is minimal, i.e. between teeth, along the gum line and under the gums.

► As plaque matures, disease-producing potential increases.

► Mature bacterial plaque will incorporate minerals into the mass, creating a hard substance called tartar or calculus.

► Disrupting the process of plaque formation before it reaches disease-causing potential is the best defense strategy.

► During early stages of formation, plaque can be disrupted by home oral hygiene techniques; once it has matured and/or mineralized it needs to be removed by a professional.

Self Checks for Oral Cancer

With the rising incidence of all forms of cancer, it is important to remember the risks and try to reduce them on a daily basis. Risk factors for cancer include the following:

► poor diet (high in fats and low in fruits and vegetables)
► use of tobacco (both smoked and smokeless)
► excessive use of alcohol
► overexposure to the sun.

Everyone can and should perform self examinations on a regular basis. The most successful management of cancer relies on early detection of malignant lesions. If any findings of self examination are suspicious, check with a medical or dental practitioner. S/he can determine whether the finding is normal or should be investigated further.

Warning signs of oral cancer include:

► A new growth, swelling or lump discovered in the soft tissues of the mouth or neck; it may or may not be painful.

► Patches on the soft tissues of the mouth which appear white and scaly or red and velvety.

► Any sore in the mouth or on the skin of the face or neck which does not heal properly within a two-week time frame.

► Persistent unusual numbness or tingling.

► Excessive dryness or wetness of tissues.

► Prolonged voice hoarseness or feeling of a "lump in the throat".

► Persistent sore throat or cough.

► Difficulty with swallowing.

► Difficulty with opening the mouth.

If any of these signs are noted, seek advice from a physician or dental professional.

Part V

An Ounce of Prevention

Chapter 9
Food Choices and Oral Health

In This Chapter

▶ diet and dental disease
▶ dental disease and host resistance
▶ fluoride – its use and abuse

Diet and Dental Disease

Proper nutrition has an important influence on oral health from conception through old age. A diet rich in all essential nutrients (vitamins, minerals and protein) is required during pregnancy so that the fetus develops normally. The quality of body tissues formed in the developing child depends on an adequate supply of the building blocks of life. For teeth and bones, this means sufficient amounts of protein and minerals. On their own, these substances cannot create healthy bodies. A variety of vitamins and trace elements are required to facilitate incorporation of basic nutrients into developing tissues.

The primary or baby teeth begin developing before birth. For complete information on the chronology of the dentition please see *Chapter 7*. From birth to the early teens, permanent teeth form and gradually replace the primary set. This process continues the need for good nutrition. Once teeth are formed and calcified there is no bodily process which will cause a tooth to "soften", demineralize or decay. Tooth tissue destruction comes from outside forces.

Frequently women will comment to their dental care providers that "my teeth were fine until I started having children but the babies robbed the calcium from my teeth and they decayed." While many women may experience an increase in dental disease during pregnancy, it is **not the fault of the fetus**. Tooth decay and gum disease are not inevitable side effects of pregnancy. *Chapter 11* describes the risk factors in detail and provides strategies for reducing them.

Once the tooth crown is fully formed and it emerges into the mouth it is vulnerable to attack. Again, diet plays a pivotal role. Three things are required to decay a tooth – bacteria (which live constantly in the mouth), food (required by bacteria as well as people) and the tooth itself.

Think for a moment about food. Many popular foods are made of carbohydrates (sugars and starches) and proteins. As far as oral bacteria are concerned, they prefer to skip the proteins and go straight for the sugar.

When colonies of bacteria consume sugar, the acid waste is held tightly against the tooth where it removes minerals from the enamel surface. Organized bacterial plaque is not easily penetrated by saliva or other fluids. It is, however, easily penetrated by sugar in solution. After eating any meal or snack containing carbohydrates, it takes the saliva about 20 minutes to penetrate the bacterial mass and neutralize the acid. Meanwhile, the acid has been eating away at tooth enamel.

Every time sugar is eaten, an "acid attack" occurs. Simple math indicates that the more often sugary foods are ingested, the longer teeth are bathed in decay-producing acid. As far as dental health is concerned, frequency of sugar exposure is more harmful than the amount eaten at any one time.

The form of sugar can contribute to the length of the acid attacks as well. A sweetened beverage drunk relatively quickly causes the sugar to pass through the mouth and the saliva can begin to neutralize the acid in the plaque. If a sweet drink is sipped over prolonged periods, the acid level in plaque remains dangerously high. Prolonged acid attacks also occur when carbohydrates in sticky form such as toffee or dried fruit are eaten. Some people routinely suck breath mints, cough drops or other slowly dissolving sugary items.

Carbohydrates are a necessary part of a balanced diet. Most people are also very fond of them. You can have your cake and keep your teeth too by restricting the intake of carbohydrates to three or four times per day. This is one way to modify a diet to improve dental health.

Foods for General and Dental Health

There are many excellent books on nutrition and health. This book is not intended to be one of them. A few more comments about diet and health, however, are warranted.

Many people eat far more carbohydrates than is good for either their bodies or their teeth. While frequency of sugar intake is a key factor in dental health, the total amount consumed creates other metabolic effects. High-carbohydrate diets can lead to sugar addiction. Once hooked, it takes increasing amounts of sugar to obtain satisfaction. Sugar junkies should attempt to substitute carbohydrate foods with those which supply protein, vitamins and minerals.

High-carbohydrate diets increase blood sugar and encourage overproduction of insulin to keep levels within normal range. Elevated blood insulin can have other negative effects on metabolism. At the very least, if energy output does not burn the available sugar in the bloodstream, it is stored as fat for future use. Obesity is becoming an ever increasing health care concern in North America and in many industrialized countries.

During puberty, high-sugar diets in combination with changing hormone levels can contribute to skin problems which plague teenagers. Dealing with acne, in addition to all the other stresses of growing up, is one thing a teenager can do without.

Nutrition in a Nutshell

For adequate general and dental health your daily diet should consist of:

► adequate high quality protein from: meats, fish, eggs, cheese, milk, tofu, legumes and nuts

► balanced amounts of carbohydrates from: whole grain breads and cereals, rice, fruits, vegetables and small amounts of sugar (as unrefined as possible, i.e. honey, maple syrup and brown sugar)

► appropriate amounts of fat from natural sources such as: meat, fish, dairy products, non-hydrogenated vegetable oils.

For good dental health, carbohydrates should be restricted to three main meals. This restriction limits the decay-producing acid attacks to a total of one hour per day. Our defense system (the mineral content in our saliva) has 23 hours to remineralize any minor tooth enamel damage which has occurred.

Restricting food intake to three times a day is probably unrealistic. Everyone likes a snack. Keeping a supply of healthy snack foods handy reduces the temptation to snack dangerously and will help quell the "growlies" and see you through a busy day.

No one is saying you can never indulge in pure "junk food" now and again. If your body doesn't need that indulgence, your psyche does. Satisfy your occasional craving and don't feel guilty. To stay in good general and dental health, the goal is not to do it on a regular basis. A healthy diet provides balanced nutrition to the body and helps diminish cravings.

Snack Facts

Before snacking: **stop**, **think**, and then **choose wisely**.

Table 9.1 Snack Choices		
BAD	**BETTER**	**BEST**
These snack foods are dangerous to dental health and provide little or no nutrition to the body.	These snack foods are dangerous to dental health but provide some useful nutrients to the body.	These snack foods are safe for teeth and some of them provide essential nutrients to the body.
candy (in any form) pastries (pies, cakes, cookies, donuts, etc.) regular soft drinks and colas sugar-sweetened teas and coffee chewing gum sweetened with sugar	real fruit juices dried fruits (drying concentrates their sugar content, changes the texture and causes them to stick to teeth) nut butters with added sugar sweetened dairy products (chocolate milk, ice cream, yogurt) plain snack crackers and potato chips coated nuts and seeds	raw fruits and vegetables cheese plain nuts and seeds nuts-only butters (such as peanut, cashew, etc.) chewing gum sweetened with sugar substitutes spring or soda water with a twist of lemon or lime

Certainly making wise food choices will go a long way to maintaining your dental health. There are other strategies related to diet which also help reduce your risk of dental decay.

Dental Disease and Host Resistance

Obviously teeth themselves are one of the factors in dental decay. People vary in their levels of susceptibility to disease. Tooth decay is no exception. This differing degree of susceptibility is referred to as host resistance. Increasing host resistance to disease is another way of reducing risk.

Although you are not born with a natural immunity to the bacteria which cause dental diseases, you do possess individual characteristics which influence the virulence (disease-producing capacity) of bacterial plaque. These factors include:

▶ The timing of eruption of teeth. Children whose teeth emerge into the mouth earlier than the average tend to be more susceptible to tooth decay.

▶ The alignment of teeth in the dental arches. Crowded or crooked teeth are more difficult to clean which gives bacteria a more favourable environment in which to organize and initiate dental disease.

▶ The amount and chemical composition of saliva. People differ in the acid-base balance (pH level) of the saliva they produce. Individuals with more basic pH saliva can neutralize plaque acids more readily. Greater saliva flow also facilitates acid neutralization.

▶ The degree to which tooth tissues are mineralized. This is influenced by genetics and the availability of proper nutrients: higher mineral content means lower tissue solubility in bacterial acids.

The only host resistance factor that can be influenced significantly is the last one. The discovery of the role of fluoride is, to date, the most important finding in the battle to increase host resistance to tooth decay.

Fluoride – Its Use and Abuse

The discovery of the benefits of fluoride in reducing tooth decay began in 1908. Dr. F.S. McKay, an American dentist, observed that a number of his clients experienced less tooth decay than average but had mottled tooth enamel. All of them lived in Colorado Springs or El Paso County. He named the abnormal tooth colouration seen in these clients "Colorado Brown Stain".

Through interviews and by the process of elimination, he discovered the common factor among the members of this group was the source of their drinking water. Repeated water analysis at that time did not uncover anything unusual. McKay was not convinced, however, and he encouraged families whose teeth were affected to seek alternative sources of drinking water. Over time, their descendants did not display the tooth discolouration of their parents.

By 1931 water analysis techniques had become more sophisticated. Now repeated analyses of the water sources previously used by McKay's clients who exhibited Colorado Brown Stain uncovered fluoride as a common element. This discolouration of tooth enamel is now called fluorosis, and it has been determined that availability of too much fluoride in the body during tooth development is the culprit.

Additional scientific studies during the 1930s and '40s established a relationship between levels of fluoride in drinking water and reduced incidence of tooth decay – without tooth enamel disfigurement. The results were reliable whether the water was naturally fluoridated or was artificially adjusted to optimal levels. "Optimal levels" are defined as approximately one part of fluoride per million parts of water (1 ppm). There is some variation in this figure based on climate conditions. Hotter climate cities reduce the amount of fluoride added because people tend to drink more water during warmer weather.

While not without controversy, fluoridation of community water supplies has allowed millions of people to enjoy better dental health.

Fluoride – Its Use

The most beneficial effect of fluoride is as previously described: taken systemically as a trace element in the diet. When it is available in this form during tooth calcification, minute amounts are incorporated into the crystalline structure of the enamel tissue. Enamel containing fluoride crystals is significantly less soluble in acids.

The easiest way to obtain optimal levels of dietary fluoride is through the use of fluoridated water. **For people using drinking water without optimal natural or adjusted fluoride levels, dietary supplements are available, by prescription, in tablet or liquid form. These should be used only as directed.**

What if you grew up without this dietary benefit? Dental researchers asked that question decades ago and found some interesting answers. Thousands of research studies have shown that various fluoride compounds applied to the tooth surface also increase the resistance of enamel to decay. This is called "topical application" of fluoride.

Initially, topical fluoride compounds were reserved for prescribed application by dental professionals. After additional research, less concentrated forms were (and still are) marketed for home use as toothpastes and mouthwashes.

Fluoride – Its Abuse

Fluoride's ability to increase resistance to tooth decay has been an enormous public health benefit. Community water fluoridation is still one of the most cost effective ways to combat a disease with almost universal prevalence.

The use of fluoride, however, has not been without its problems. People are inclined to think that if a little is good, then more is better. In the case of fluoride, too much can result in dental complications. Unfortunately, as the access to fluoride has increased, so has the incidence of dental fluorosis.

Current guidelines for the use of fluoride supplements in all forms prevent users from receiving too much of a good thing.

Canadian Dental Association – Policy on Fluorides

▶ Dietary fluoride supplements are recommended only for individuals or groups at **high risk** for dental decay where the estimated amount of fluoride ingested from all sources indicates a need.

▶ Estimation of fluoride ingestion should include all water sources used routinely and the possible impact of water filtration devices connected with the water supply.

▶ Fluoride supplement dosages for high-risk individuals or groups are based on chronological age and the fluoride level of their usual water supply.

▶ Chewable tablets or lozenges are the preferred forms of supplement administration; drops may be used for individuals requiring special care.

Table 9.2 Systemic Fluoride Supplement Doses for Identified Groups at High Risk for Caries (Tooth Decay) - (As prescribed under Canadian Dental Association Guidelines)	
Daily Supplement Dose	
Age	**Fluoride in Water Supply less than 0.3 ppm**
younger than 3 years	not recommended
3, 4, 5 years	0.25 mg if fluoride toothpaste is used regularly 0.5 mg if fluoride toothpaste is **not** used regularly
6-13 years	1.0 mg

The Canadian Dental Association also includes in its fluoride policies guidelines for a more conservative use of topically applied fluoride. These include:

▶ restriction of professional fluoride treatments to high-risk clients at all ages

▶ no professional topical application of fluorides for children under 6 years of age

▶ no community health topical fluoride programs for children under 6 years of age

▶ restriction of the amount of fluoride toothpaste children use to a "pea-sized" dose on the toothbrush

▶ adult supervision of children who are brushing their teeth until they are old enough and responsible enough not to be tempted to swallow the paste.

Chapter 10
Attack That Plaque

In This Chapter

► enamel sealants

► chemical plaque control

► mechanical plaque control

► checklist for first-time flossers

► tongue hygiene

Enamel Sealants

Chapter 9 details the role of diet in dental disease and how to use food choices to increase resistance to tooth decay. It also describes the concept of increasing "host resistance" to disease and the use of fluoride to do so. Another method of preventing dental disease by increasing host resistance is by placing enamel sealants on teeth at greatest risk for decay.

The discovery of plastic materials which can bond with tooth enamel provides another means of preventing tooth decay. The teeth at greatest risk are those with deep pits and grooves, especially on their biting surfaces. The teeth best answering this description are the permanent molars and premolars. Also, they appear in the mouth from about six to 13 years of age, a time when their owners' oral hygiene practices may be less than perfect but their ability to co-operate with simple dental procedures is adequate. The procedure to place enamel sealants is described in *Chapter 6*.

Teeth that are ideal candidates for a sealant are:

► newly erupted (i.e. have been in place in the mouth for only a short time)

► free of decay on all surfaces (not just the one to be sealed).

Children who are ideal candidates for sealant procedures:

► must be old enough and well motivated to co-operate adequately.

Successful placement of enamel sealants is technique sensitive. This means each stage of the operation has to be performed optimally, which requires excellent client co-operation. Although primary molars also have grooves and pits fitting the tooth eligibility criteria listed, practitioners would be dealing with children two to three years of age. Children this young do not have the motivation, attention span and muscle control to be compliant participants in the placement process. Also, the enamel composition of primary teeth differs somewhat from permanent teeth and sealant retention is less reliable. For these reasons, most practitioners do not routinely recommend enamel sealants for primary teeth.

Chemical Plaque Control

Attacking the third link in the chain, bacterial plaque, is the final step in dental disease prevention.

Although much fuss is made in advertisements about products which "kill 90 percent of harmful oral bacteria", you need to look carefully at these claims. Most chemicals designed to rid the mouth of bacteria have two basic characteristics:

▶ They tend to be non-selective in their effects so they eliminate both harmful and non-disease-producing bacteria with equal efficiency.

▶ The effects are temporary, lasting from a few minutes to a few hours.

There is certainly a place for use of bactericidal products in the quest for oral health. They should not be viewed, however, as a panacea for solving all dental disease problems. At this stage of development their potential for providing a long-term solution to plaque control is limited.

The human body lives in harmony with vast numbers of bacteria. Many of them are, if not downright beneficial, at least harmless under most circumstances. Even many of the disease-producing strains are kept in check if the immune system is operating normally.

Species which are beneficial or harmless are referred to as the *normal bacterial flora*. Introducing a chemical designed to eliminate bacteria runs the risk of disturbing the delicate balance of species that make up the normal flora. When this balance is disturbed there is increased risk of harm to tissues caused by rampant growth of bacteria that normally would be harmless.

Experience with antibiotics over the last several decades has lead to wariness of their overuse. The prevalence of these products has assisted the evolution of strains of bacteria resistant to many currently identified antibiotic treatments. The appearance of so-called "super bugs" can pose a real threat to well being.

For these reasons, chemical control of oral bacteria over the long term is not a preferred option for most people. Fortunately, other less potentially dangerous methods of plaque control are available.

Mechanical Plaque Control

You knew it was coming – the message about brushing and flossing. Like it or not, this is still the most effective, long-term, least risky option for maintaining oral health.

How many times have you heard the exhortation, "brush your teeth after eating", and felt guilty because you couldn't always do it? Relax, safe in the knowledge that brushing between bites is not a strategy that will keep teeth and gums healthy.

To prevail in the battle with bacteria, it is important to "know the enemy". Oral bacteria live in huge numbers in the mouth all the time. When floating around in random fashion, they do little harm. It is only as they organize into sticky, compact masses that they produce acids and toxic waste in sufficient quantities to harm tissues. It takes bacteria about 24 hours to organize into disease-producing plaque. This characteristic allows you to restrict your plaque-fighting activities to an all-out assault once a day. Any additional opportunities you have to disturb bacteria are a bonus.

Note the advice is not "brush your teeth once a day." Bacteria are sneaky. They tend to colonize in areas where they are least likely to be disturbed – by toothbrushes or anything else. Methods to stir them up on a daily basis will be as individual as your own mouth. The goal is not total elimination of the germs but rather to keep them in a constant state of relative disorganization.

Plaque-conquering Devices – Toothbrushes

Any item which achieves the goal of bacterial disruption without doing damage to the soft or hard tissues in the mouth is fair game. The most common tool for cleaning teeth is the lowly toothbrush. As you know, toothbrushes come in a mind-boggling variety of shapes, sizes, textures, colours and as manual or powered models. Choose one that is going to work best for you, bearing in mind the following principles:

▶   Make sure it is the correct size for your mouth. The brush head should fit lengthwise on the tongue side of your lower front teeth without tufts of bristles hanging over the teeth at the corners

▶ The bristles, whatever their arrangement on the brush head, should be soft, flexible under gentle pressure and rounded at the tips so they don't scratch the soft tissues

▶ The handle should feel comfortable in your hand and provide access for the head to all areas of your mouth.

Regardless of how innovative the design of a toothbrush, it will still reach only three of the five surfaces of each tooth. Some additional devices will be required to disrupt the plaque forming on the side surfaces of adjacent teeth (the interproximal areas). More information is provided about these later.

If you have chosen your brush according to the principles above, and apply it to tooth surfaces with gentle pressure and short vibrating or circular motions, you are likely to disrupt plaque without damaging tissues. There are many weird and wonderful prescribed ways of brushing the teeth. Many of the methods bear the names of dentists who invented those techniques eons ago. If you consider principles of brushing, you can adopt a unique style which is required to do the job in your mouth.

When you brush your teeth:

▶ Brush first using only water. Foaming, fresh-tasting toothpaste makes you feel as if you have done a good job even when you haven't. If you brush only with water your tongue will know right away whether or not your teeth are "squeaky clean".

▶ Start with the areas hardest to reach so they should get maximum attention. For most people these areas are: the tongue side of the lower back teeth; behind the lower front teeth (tongue side) and the cheek side of the upper back teeth. Once these are done, no one will forget to brush the places that show.

▶ In every area, concentrate the majority of the brushing effort on the third of the teeth closest to the gums. This is where the plaque accumulates most heavily. Angle the bristles towards the gums and gently encourage them to slide slightly under the soft tissue.

▶ Once the brush head is properly placed, move the brush back and forth slightly or in a tiny circular motion. The aim is to flex the bristles against the teeth to disrupt plaque. Keep the motion subtle – don't scrub.

▶ When one area is complete move the brush head to the adjacent teeth, making sure to overlap with the previous area so that no tooth surfaces have been missed.

▶ Be methodical. Develop a routine. Do the same areas in the same order each time so that you brush all accessible surfaces thoroughly.

▶ Take your time. The process can't be rushed and still be effective. Probably you are not currently spending enough time brushing your teeth. A thorough brushing job should take two to four minutes depending on the characteristics of your dentition and your level of dexterity. **Complete oral hygiene procedures** need to be done only once a day to maintain health. You are free to brush and floss more often if you want, but **thorough** cleaning once a day is a must!

Interproximal Cleaning – Dental Floss

Interproximal is a fancy word to describe the sides of teeth which face each other in the same arch. Disturbing plaque here is a challenge.

Enter dental floss. It is designed to scrape bacterial plaque from the sides of the teeth above and below the gum line. Although you will find it cumbersome to manipulate at first, it is still the most useful interproximal cleaning aid for most people.

This specialized string comes in a variety of thicknesses, textures and even flavours. Table 10.1 summarizes the characteristics of floss available and the general uses for each. Experiment to find a type of floss that suits your needs and abilities.

No one will tell you learning to floss your teeth is easy! Neither was tying your shoes for the first time. With a will and some perseverance, you too can learn to floss effectively.

As with brushing, stick to the principles outlined. Since a picture is reportedly worth a thousand words, check the diagrams in figure 10.1 for better understanding.

▶ Control the floss by wrapping it around your middle fingers. Keep the thumbs and forefingers free to guide the floss into position. The floss will be under adequate control when your thumbs and forefingers are about 3 cm (1 inch) apart.

▶ To reach the target area of the teeth, you must guide the floss past the point where adjacent teeth contact each other. Your contacts may vary on a scale from loose to incredibly tight. Either way, see-saw the floss back and forth until it slides through. Don't snap the floss through quickly. This is not only uncomfortable, it can also damage the soft tissue.

▶ Wrap the floss in a "C" shape against one side of one tooth.

▶ Rub the floss several times up and down that tooth surface from below the gum line to the contact point.

▶ Stop at the contact area, direct the "C" of floss against the side of the adjacent tooth and repeat the step above. Be careful not to catch the flap of gum tissue as you change direction.

▶ Remove the floss through the contact area. If you have extremely tight contacts which tend to shred the floss, unwrap the floss from the finger on the tongue side. Pull the floss out of the space below the contact and towards your cheek.

▶ Select a clean area on the floss and move on to the next pair of teeth. Continue until all proximal surfaces are clean. Don't forget to loop the floss around the back surfaces of the last teeth in the arches as well.

Fig. 10.1A.

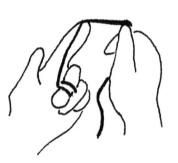

Fig. 10.1B.

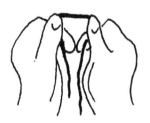

Views A, B and C illustrate hand positions to control floss.

Fig. 10.1C.

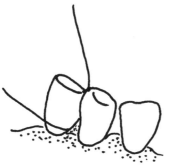

Fig. 10.1D. Adapt floss to one side of one tooth.

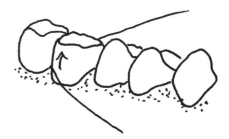

Fig. 10.1E. Slide floss under gums.

Fig. 10.1F. Scrape floss along the tooth surface from the gum line towards the biting surface.

Table 10.1 Types of Dental Floss		
Type of Dental Floss	**Advantages**	**Indications for Use**
standard un-waxed	▸ comes in a variety of thicknesses depending on manufacturer	▸ snug or loose contacts ▸ requires average or above manual dexterity
standard waxed	▸ slides through contacts more easily ▸ less slippery to control	▸ dentitions with tight contacts ▸ requires lower level of dexterity to control
shred resistant	▸ less likely to shred or break	▸ easier to use where numerous interproximal fillings in sides of teeth tend to shred average floss
plastic-type floss or tape	▸ described by manufacturers as "easy or glide through" ▸ easiest type to slip through contact points between teeth	▸ dentitions with very tight contacts with or without interproximal fillings ▸ because it tends to be slippery, requires higher levels of dexterity to control
thick and thin floss	▸ floss with alternating thin sections and foam-like thicker sections ▸ thin sections slide through contacts, thicker areas are used to disturb plaque	▸ use where periodontal disease has destroyed some bone between teeth ▸ excellent for disturbing plaque where more surface area of the teeth is exposed

Checklist for First-time Flossers

▶   Choose a type of floss from table 10.1 which you think is most appropriate to your needs. Don't hesitate to switch types if it seems helpful to do so.

▶   Plan to begin learning to floss when you can accommodate the following:

Schedule 10 to 20 consecutive days when you can set aside sufficient time to practise in a relaxed atmosphere.

Give yourself lots of time at each attempt (at least 10 minutes at first).

Don't get frustrated; you will probably find flossing very awkward for awhile.

Start with the front teeth, then work your way back to the posterior ones.

Don't skip any days while you are learning – that only prolongs the acquisition of the skill.

▶   Always work carefully in a controlled manner.

▶   Work with a mirror at first. Eventually you will want to be able to floss without it. Flossing by feel alone means you can fit it into your busy schedule more easily.

▶   If you are a first-time flosser, don't be surprised if your gums bleed. Bleeding is a sign that tissues are diseased where plaque has been accumulating undisturbed. As you get more proficient at disturbing the plaque in these areas, the tissues will heal and the bleeding will stop. For many people this may take seven to 14 days.

▶   For first-timers, flossing may become uncomfortable about day two or three. Check your technique to make sure it is sound. Remember, the tissues have not been healthy. As they heal, there will be some discomfort just as with any bruise or minor skin abrasion.   Persevere; this too will pass. If you abandon your efforts at this point and resume flossing at a later date, you will only have to go through this phase again.

▶   As your skill improves, your time investment each day will become less. Eventually you should be able to do a thorough job of flossing and brushing in three to five minutes per day.

▶   Anticipate the rewards of your efforts:

fresher breath
healthier gums
easier professional dental cleanings
fewer cavities
lower dental bills

▶ If, after giving flossing your best shot, it really is not going to work for you, check the other suggestions for interproximal cleaning offered in *Chapter 12* of this section.

Tongue Hygiene

You may be fastidious about cleaning your teeth and gums but your oral care isn't complete until you attend to tongue hygiene. Just as bacteria rest and flourish in recesses around teeth and gingival tissues, they lurk and breed in the depressions and fissures of the tongue. Since the goal of oral self care is to reduce the number of bacteria and increase the level of disruption of bacterial plaque, the tongue as a source of plaque needs regular attention.

Tongues usually are not considered to be things of beauty. If they are obviously coated with bacterial plaque which may become stained with food dyes or tobacco products they can be downright disgusting. This problem could be considered another good reason to try to quit smoking. Coated tongues can leave a foul taste in their owner's mouth and also contribute to less than sweet breath.

Lately a number of special devices have been marketed to clean the tongue. Some toothbrushes are now designed with tongue cleaners on the back of the brushing head. Try them and if you find one you like use it regularly. You don't need to get fancy devices to do the job. After brushing your teeth, simply apply the brush to your tongue. Reach as far back as your gag reflex allows (you will get more tolerant of tongue brushing if you persist). Rinse your mouth and the brush thoroughly to flush out loosened debris and you're done.

Complete daily plaque-control routines allow you to enjoy great health returns on your investments of a small financial outlay for supplies and a few minutes time each day.

Chapter 11
Oral Health for a Lifetime

In This Chapter

- ► devices and strategies for plaque control for people of all ages
- ► plaque-control strategies for dependent persons
- ► tooth loss and pregnancy: myths debunked
- ► oral self care during orthodontic treatment
- ► denture care
- ► maintaining your motivation
- ► regular professional assistance
- ► bruxism (teeth-grinding habit)
- ► tooth safety

Devices and Strategies for Plaque Control for People of All Ages

Oral Hygiene for Infants

It is amazing how many adults, who don't turn a hair at changing a smelly diaper, get suddenly squeamish when they are advised to clean their infants' mouths. New parents need to realize oral hygiene is as important to a baby's health as cleanliness of any other part of the body. For baby, mouth cleaning should be as much a part of daily routine as a bath and should start as early.

The reason mouth care begins even before the teeth emerge is to teach children it is all right for an adult to perform oral care for them. Once teeth erupt, daily oral hygiene is necessary to prevent disease. When routine mouth cleaning is established in infancy, children will be more accepting of adult assistance until they are competent to do a thorough job for themselves. For most children this will not be until they are nine or 10 years of age.

The main rule in oral hygiene practices for infants and preschool children is to **keep it simple**. Before teeth erupt into the mouth a, gentle sweep over the gum pads after nursing is all that is required. Use your forefinger wrapped in a clean, damp wash cloth or gauze square. A few seconds is all it takes. The key is to make it routine so *you* don't forget and the *child learns to expect and accept* the activity.

When the first few teeth arrive, the only change in routine is to be sure you are gently polishing the facial and the tongue sides of the teeth. Until the molars erupt, use of the cloth or gauze is sufficient. Once the molars are in place, a small, very soft toothbrush is appropriate. By this time (18-24 months of age) your child will be interested in imitating brushing which he sees adults doing on a regular basis.

Encourage your child to try brushing. It is evidence of your child's growth towards independence. It often accompanies the "terrible twos". Don't abdicate your responsibility for doing the thorough job required to maintain health. Kids chewing on toothbrushes can make great pictures but their efforts are no match for the power of plaque.

When the primary molar teeth emerge (about 20-30 months of age) oral hygiene for tots becomes a bit more complex both physically and psychologically. With 20 primary teeth in place, eight of them with broad side and chewing surfaces, a damp cloth is no longer going to be an adequate plaque deterrent. There are too many nooks and crannies in which bacteria can lodge and organize.

Children's primary teeth are normally distributed around the dental arches in one of four predictable patterns. For a complete discussion of the possibilities please see *Chapter 7*. Some children have wide spaces between some or all of the adjacent teeth in each arch while some have arches where teeth are arranged in contact with the ones on either side. Teeth arranged without spaces between them are more challenging to clean. Remember, bacteria organize into decay-producing plaque in areas where they are least likely to be disturbed. In a toddler's mouth, those areas are between adjacent teeth which are in contact and in the grooves of the molars.

For exposed tooth surfaces, a small, soft toothbrush is appropriate to disturb plaque. Use it damp. Toothpaste is not necessary: its use can be delayed until the child is old enough to understand it should not be swallowed and is physically capable of spitting it out. If you want to introduce your young child to toothpaste, choose a specially formulated one **without fluoride**. If some of it is swallowed it does not pose a risk. Press gently on the brush and clean all exposed surfaces using a tiny circular scrubbing motion. Scrub biting surfaces last.

If adjacent molars are in contact, a toothbrush is not sufficient. Dental floss comes to the rescue. This is a job for adults only. You will probably find lightly waxed dental floss is the easiest to manage. Take a piece of floss about 18 inches (45 cm) in length. Wrap it snugly around the middle fingers of each hand. Use your thumbs and forefingers to guide the floss. For better understanding of the process, see figure 10.1 in *Chapter 10*.

When working in your child's mouth, keep about 1 inch (about 3 cm) of floss stretched between your forefingers. Slide the floss carefully between the molars, using a see-saw motion, until it is below the point of contact. Wrap it in a "C" shape against the side of one tooth and wipe the plaque towards the biting surface of the tooth. Repeat the procedure for the side of the adjacent tooth.

Always start with the molar teeth. They are the ones most vulnerable to decay and are the ones your child will keep the longest. Do as many of the areas as your child's co-operation will allow. To be effective it needs to be done only once a day! Even a few times a week is better than not at all.

If you find that you are all fingers and thumbs when trying to floss your child's teeth, try using a floss-holding device or a small disposable flosser shown in figures 12.2 and 12.3 in *Chapter 12*.

By now all you parents are asking how this is remotely possible for a squirming two-year-old. If you have made oral care a part of your child's routine from the beginning, you will have less difficulty, even through the "terrible twos" and beyond.

Toddlers' "Hints for Hygiene" Checklist

▶ Make adult-assisted oral hygiene a routine from the very beginning

▶ Keep the techniques as simple, effective and as much fun as possible.

▶ Always clean the most vulnerable areas of the child's mouth first while co-operation is at its peak.

▶ Always accommodate your child's level of co-operation. Some days will be better than others. Be firm and friendly in your approach. Never allow oral care assistance to become a contest of wills between you and your child. If it is a bad day for your child, do the minimal, but do something. Praise for co-operation at the level it is offered and aim for better results next time. It is important not to break the habits being established.

▶ As your child's capabilities increase, encourage "brushing" once a day by her/himself. Don't forget to do a thorough job for her/him at least once a day (preferably at bedtime).

▶ As the child grows, try positioning yourself on a sofa or bed with the child lying with his head in your lap. By age three or four years, you may find it easier to sit and have him lean against your lower legs, head tipped back in your lap.

▶ Enjoy the fruits of your labours: cleaner, healthier teeth for your child and lower dental bills for you to pay.

Children Four to Five Years of Age

This is the age when most children begin a new adventure – school. It is one of the first milestones in your child's growing independence. By now, the habit of having a clean mouth should be well established. If your child's early efforts at "tooth brushing" have been encouraged, s/he should be able to move on to a more efficient technique. Usually at this age children can handle a technique known in the dental field as the Fones method (after American dentist Alfred C. Fones).

To do this, the child closes the teeth together and brushes the facial sides of the teeth with large circular strokes. Encourage working from one back end of the arches around to the other. When all facial surfaces have been brushed, the next areas are done with the mouth open. Scrub back and forth on the biting surfaces of the molar teeth, upper and lower. Usually, children's co-ordination dictates that during this activity, the brush will accidentally do some cleaning of the tongue side of the back teeth as well. This is a happy coincidence.

In recognition of the child's growing independence, s/he should be encouraged to brush (with some casual adult supervision) at least once a day. Perhaps this could be established as a routine after breakfast before going to school. Parents need to reserve the right to do complete oral hygiene procedures (brushing and flossing as described earlier) once each day. Bedtime is preferred. However, fit it into the daily routine as appropriate. As long as plaque is well disrupted once every 24 hours, the health benefits accrue.

Toothpaste is not necessary. Effective plaque disruption can occur using a wet brush. If toothpaste does encourage your child to brush more regularly and efficiently, use one that supports this habit. Remember, use only a "pea-sized" amount on the brush. Remind the child to "spit out; don't swallow."

Oral Hygiene Checklist for Four- and Five-Year-Old Children

▶ Encourage independent brushing once a day under casual adult supervision.

▶ Maintain the habit of brushing and flossing once a day by an adult.

▶ Introduce toothpaste. Make sure the child is spitting it out, not swallowing it. Use only a "pea-sized" amount on the brush. Choose a paste containing fluoride if it is appropriate (see guidelines on use of fluoride in *Chapter 9*).

▸   Monitor your child's increasing capabilities to determine readiness for greater responsibility for oral care.

Children Six to Ten Years of Age

This age range heralds another milestone in dental development – the arrival of permanent teeth. Usually first in the sequence are the first of the permanent molars. Due to the timing of their appearance they are also called "six-year-old" molars. They erupt behind the last primary teeth in the arches. Many parents think these are still baby teeth. Not only are they permanent, but they are the foundations of occlusion in the adult dentition. For details, please see *Chapter 7*.

The arrival of the molars is closely followed by the central incisors. By their sixth holiday season, most children can justifiably sing, "All I want for Chrithmath ith my two front teeth." Not only are children growing, they are increasingly mastering their bodies.

Large-muscle co-ordination which allowed independent locomotion continues to be refined. Small muscles are now following suit. At school, printing skills improve and by eight or nine years of age, children begin to write. Once these manual skills are undertaken, children are ready to move on to a more sophisticated brushing technique.

The method recommended is known as "rolling stroke". This method emphasizes brushing teeth in the direction in which they grow. It is designed to effect more thorough cleaning. It also provides a foundation for brush motions important in cleaning a complete adult dentition while protecting the soft gum tissues.

Rolling-stroke brushing is done in each arch separately. The lower teeth are brushed "up" from gum line to biting surface. The upper teeth are brushed down. Biting surfaces are scrubbed in a back and forth motion. Younger children can be reminded of the pattern using a little jingle:

> Up like the flowers.
> Down like the rain.
> Back and forth
> Like a choo-choo train.

Use the brush at a 45-degree angle, beginning just over the gums. Begin at one end of the arch and work around to the other end. In each area press gently and roll the brush up the tooth from the gums to the biting edge of the teeth. Move the brush to the adjacent area, making sure to overlap with the area just completed. Do a minimum of five strokes in each brush position.

Once one side (facial or tongue) of that arch has been brushed, return around the same arch on the opposite side. Complete the second arch in the same manner. All the biting surfaces are scrubbed last.

Earlier in this section parents were advised to begin oral hygiene procedures with teeth most vulnerable to disease. Children should be coached to begin brushing in the areas hardest to clean. That way, maximum attention goes where it will be most beneficial. Sequence is important. Encourage your child to develop a habit of brushing teeth in the same order making sure no areas are skipped.

A suggested sequence that follows all of the principles above would be:

▶ Begin on the **tongue side of the lower teeth**.

▶ Work from one end of the arch around to the other.

▶ Move to the facial side of the lower teeth and work back around the arch to finish at the end where you began.

▶ Repeat the procedures on the **upper teeth beginning on the facial surfaces** and returning along the arch on the sides of the teeth facing the palate.

▶ Brush the biting surfaces of the lower teeth and then the upper teeth.

▶ Brush the tongue.

▶ Rinse the mouth thoroughly.

▶ Rinse the brush well.

It is a fact of life that girls develop physically at an earlier age than boys. The timing of tooth eruption and the development of small-muscle co-ordination fit this pattern. By eight or nine years of age girls usually can be encouraged to begin using dental floss. Boys may not be ready to take this step until they are 10 or 11. By happy coincidence children's manual dexterity often develops about the time the permanent teeth are present in an arrangement which makes them easier to floss!

By nine or 10 years of age, most children have eight permanent front teeth (four in the upper arch and four in the lower). Four permanent molars are the last teeth in the back of both arches. The permanent canine teeth may be appearing at the corners of the lower arch and some of the adjacent primary molar teeth may be slightly loose. For more complete information of the sequence and timing of tooth eruption, please see *Chapter 7*.

If children have been assisted and coached through dental hygiene procedures since birth, learning to floss is just another step along the way. Start establishing the routine by making the child responsible for flossing all the permanent front teeth. You can check the efficiency and improve the results, if necessary, when you floss the molars.

There are some tricks which make flossing easier for children. Take a piece of floss about 10 inches (25 cm) long and tie it in a circle. Allow the child to hold it in any manner which is comfortable as long as the following principles are observed:

▶ The fingers guiding the floss should be about 1 to 2 inches (3-5 cm) apart.

▶ The child can control the floss while it is inserted between the teeth and below the gums.

▶ Hand placement allows the child to wrap the floss around each side of each tooth to sweep the plaque towards the biting surfaces.

Once the child has mastered the basics on the front teeth, s/he can gradually assume responsibility for the back teeth as they are replaced by permanent ones. As manual dexterity improves, s/he will learn more convenient ways to manipulate the floss for better results.

Oral Hygiene Checklist for Children Six to Ten Years of Age

▶ At lower ages of the range children should be brushing once a day by themselves.

▶ Fluoride toothpaste may be appropriate.

▶ As small-muscle co-ordination develops, children should be coached in flossing techniques suitable to their capability. Parents still need to assist as necessary.

▶ An adult should be responsible for ensuring thorough plaque disruption is done once a day.

▶ Provide encouragement and positive reinforcement for your child's efforts.

Oral Hygiene for Preteens and Teens

The last years before the teens are heralded by many changes in physique and behaviour which can baffle children and parents alike. Puberty is the root cause for these changes. Many unpredictable responses to formerly normal events can be attributed to rapid growth and raging hormones.

You may find your preteen displays some or all of the following characteristics:

▶ A desire to engage in strenuous physical activities such as soccer, hockey, basketball, tennis, etc. Body growth dictates a need for such exercise. Try to ensure your preteen is playing safely, preferably under adult supervision. Use of appropriate equipment for face and mouth protection should be encouraged.

▶ Most preteens prefer group play at organized games and sports to individual activities.

▶ Your preteen and young teen doesn't spend most of Saturday and Sunday in bed without reason. Rapid growth and strenuous activities result in periods of sluggishness and ineptitude.

▶ Ravenous but finicky appetites are not unusual. Some children will use diet as a means of asserting independence. Even at this age, eating disorders are a potential problem. Watch for any signs that might indicate your child (particularly a daughter) may be developing unhealthy eating patterns. If you are concerned your child may be following detrimental dietary practices, seek advice from reputable professionals. Eating disorders are potentially life-threatening and require complex management for a successful outcome.

▶ Peer pressure may cause rejection of a teen's parental standards of behaviour. Children this age can be secretive about their social relationships.

▶ This is the age of exploration and transient interests: hockey one month, rock guitar the next, followed by ballet and horseback riding in rapid succession. Make sure the love affair with the activity is genuine before investing in expensive equipment!

▶ Tension and conflict can arise when standards set by adults cannot be attained by the child. The standards can be in such diverse areas as personal grooming, tidiness, honesty, privacy, earning and spending of his/her own money, etc.

► This is a period of fluctuating emotions:

    dependence on the family versus a drive for independence

    respect for parental values versus antagonism towards parental constraints

    loyalty to home versus allegiance to peer group values.

So what does all this have to do with oral health? By the age of 12, average children have the intellectual and physical capacity to be responsible for their own oral hygiene. They shouldn't even need reminding to follow suitable, established daily routines. Reminders from parents may only prove to be an ineffectual aggravation to all parties. Leave the nagging to the professionals at your child's regular dental visits. That leaves one less thing you need to nag about.

Good or bad, by this age oral hygiene habits will be well established. If the habit pattern has been ideal to good, be prepared for some backsliding as your child enters the home stretch towards independence. If the habits have been poor to date, don't expect immediate improvement.

Many preteens go through a phase which can be referred to, politely, as the "grub period". Don't be surprised if you suddenly see fewer of your preteen's articles of clothing in the laundry. Check under the bed or in a pile behind the door or in a corner of the closet. They have been placed there carefully for future use at an instant's notice.

Consumption of shampoo may drop significantly during this time and access to the bathroom may be a breeze for parents. Be patient; this too shall pass. The phase may last for a few weeks to a few months. Enjoy your reduced energy bills and freer access to bathing while you can. Soon your preteen will be a teenager and suddenly three, half-hour showers a day will be a necessity (with fresh towels required after each one).

This return to the "body clean" usually coincides with increasing interest in social relationships with the opposite gender. Hope that as a spin-off benefit, your teen expresses increased awareness of the need for oral hygiene. With luck, they will initiate appropriate tangible action on their own. Keep your lips closed and the oral hygiene supplies handy. Just enjoy your teen's return to healthy personal hygiene practices. Remember oral hygiene supplies are much cheaper than fillings.

By 13 or 14 years of age, the majority of children will have 28 of their 32 permanent teeth. This is considered to be a complete adult dentition. Third molars cannot always be accommodated within the arch length and an increasing percentage of people never develop them.

With all the permanent teeth in place, plaque control becomes most complex. Plaque forms on exposed surfaces along the gum line and extends under the gums. Heaviest accumulations are between teeth and on the tongue side of the lower back teeth and the facial side of the upper molars. Plaque left in these areas will contribute to gum and bone disease and will also increase the risk for cavities.

Most dental professionals will advise your child to adopt a more adult brushing style. The method often recommended is a modification of the rolling stroke taught at an earlier age. It could be described as the "jiggle and roll" technique.

Place the brush over the gums at a 45-degree angle. While pressing gently (enough so the gums "blanch" or turn white under the pressure), vibrate the brush to flex the bristles. This action will coax the bristles just under the gums to help disrupt plaque there. Jiggle the brush in place for several seconds. The idea is not to scrub but to create movement of the bristles to break up the plaque deposit. Sweep the brush towards the biting surface. Repeat a few times before moving to the adjacent area. Place the brush to overlap the previous area as you work your way around the arch. Using an established sequence to ensure thoroughness is important.

Remember, even the most sophisticated brushing technique will only reach three of the five tooth surfaces. Those pesky sides contacting adjacent teeth also need thorough cleaning. Perfecting the use of dental floss on a daily basis is necessary for total mouth health. Flossing techniques were described earlier in this chapter.

Parents' Checklist for Preteen and Teen Oral Hygiene

▶ Don't make oral hygiene practices a big hassle. There will be many more critical issues between you and your teen requiring your energy to resolve.

▶ Let the dental professionals whom your child sees on a regular basis get on his/her case. At this age your child is more likely to listen to them about such matters anyway.

▶ If you have done your best to establish good oral home-care habits for your child to this point, relax. Usually children will return to appropriate behaviour as they mature.

▶ Be a good listener and keep the dental hygiene aids handy.

Preteen and Teen Oral Hygiene Checklist

▶ Nobody likes a "grunge-mouth". Keep up the flossing and brushing every day.

▶ Give your parents a break by doing it on your own, without the nagging. (It's hard, but realize that your parents really do want what is best for you.)

▶ Listen to your hygienist and dentist when they give you tips to make oral care easier. (They want what is best for you too!)

▶ Act now for lifelong benefit. Although none of you plans to turn 40 anytime soon, if you make it with a healthy mouth you will thank yourself for all those hours of brushing and flossing as a teen.

Young Adults (20-30 years of age) and Oral Self Care

This is the phase during which most children make the final physical, psychological and financial break with the family. Formal education is largely completed and careers are launched. The kids relocate for independent living. This period is often complicated by student loan repayment and parenthood.

Growing up in a household that emphasized good dental health habits is great foundation for cash-strapped young adults. Keep dental bills down by keeping oral hygiene practices up. Sometimes busy schedules tend to interfere. Get back to basics in oral hygiene procedures. Two hands, a chunk of dental floss, a toothbrush, a glass of water and two or three uninterrupted minutes per day are all you really need to maintain oral health. Any additional opportunities which present for oral self care are a bonus.

Look at piggy-backing dental care procedures with another activity. Maybe you spend a few minutes at the kitchen table with the newspaper after everyone else is out of the house. Consider brushing and flossing while you read. Maybe you watch the late evening news on TV each day. Keep the floss handy by your favourite chair. During a commercial break get a glass of water and your brush to disturb that plaque. You can always do a quick whip around with the toothpaste later for the added benefits of flavour and fluoride. However, be considerate of the people who share your living space; not everyone appreciates flossing as a spectator sport.

Check your daily routines. Good oral hygiene practices can be squeezed in throughout the day. Not only are you doing great things for your own health, you are setting a good example for your children.

Mid-life Adults (30-60 years of age) and Oral Self Care

For some mid-life adults, dental care gets short shrift as other, more important, responsibilities take precedent. Some are the busy heads of single-parent families and some are part of a two-career household. Many also belong to the "sandwich generation" where demands of a growing family and aging parents leave little time for oneself.

With employment established and many employers providing dental insurance with good coverage, finding money for dental care is often less problematic than finding time for maintaining good home oral health habits. Sometimes the tendency is to keep regular appointments with your dental practitioners and hope they can compensate for your backsliding at home. The good news is you are continuing to seek assistance. The bad news is that your dentist or dental hygienist cannot, in two or three visits a year, undo the effects of daily inattention.

For most mid-life adults (particularly at the lower end of the age range) the principles of good oral health are pretty much the same as discussed for young adults above. Take a look at your opportunities for oral home care and see where it will fit best.

If, as you matured, you experienced some periodontal disease, you may find some of the oral hygiene aids discussed in the next section, make self care easier. Some of them may even save you a bit of precious time.

Older Adults (60+ years of age) and Oral Self Care

Longer periods of suffering the "slings and arrows of outrageous fortune" make older adults the most diverse population in terms of health and socio-economic status. It was stated earlier that tooth loss is not an inevitable part of aging. There are, however, a number of predictable physical changes that come with an increasing number of birthdays. These changes include:

► slower metabolism

► possible incidence of chronic diseases which are often accompanied by reduced strength and energy

► medications which may have oral side effects

► altered eating habits.

Each of these changes has an impact on oral health and its maintenance. Slower metabolism means tissues damaged by disease take longer to heal. This is particularly true for older adults with type 2 diabetes.

Various forms of arthritis zap energy and make movement a chore. Fine motor skills may diminish making oral hygiene more difficult even for the well motivated and previously highly skilled. Check the list of adaptive aids suggested in *Chapter 12* and see if some of them are right for you.

All medications, however necessary they may be, have side effects. Many types of drugs used to treat such conditions as high blood pressure, chronic pain, insomnia, psychological depression, etc. have "dry mouth" listed as a possible side effect. In addition to being uncomfortable, reduced salivary flow gives oral plaque freer rein to cause disease. Maintain the best oral hygiene possible. If your mouth is uncomfortably dry you may consider using a saliva substitute. Resist the urge to use sugar-laden candy or chewing gum. Choose sugar-free products instead. Your health care professional can provide you with advice for dealing with a chronically dry mouth.

Good nutrition is as important for seniors as it is for infants. Although there are lots of reasons for taking short cuts to meal preparation, it is important to try to eat a well-balanced diet every day at any age.

Plaque-control Strategies for Dependent Persons

Hereditary and chronic health conditions may leave individuals dependent on the assistance of others for their personal-care needs, including mouth hygiene procedures. Daily plaque control is very important as these people may not be able to report symptoms of oral disease. If disease becomes established it can cause needless suffering and possible systemic complications.

Individuals needing such assistance may fall into one or more of the following categories. Those who are:

▶ intellectually or behaviourally challenged (e.g. Down's syndrome, Alzheimer disease, autism, etc.)

▶ physically challenged by paralysis or lack of muscle control (e.g. cerebral palsy, muscular dystrophy, Parkinson's disease, strokes, etc.)

▶ unresponsive or comatose.

Suggestions to caregivers for assisting individuals with each type of dependency are discussed in detail.

Persons with Intellectual or Behavioural Challenges

Those familiar with an individual who is intellectually or behaviourally challenged will know his/her level of psychological and emotional function. Although the chronological age may be 40, the emotional and social responses may be more typical of a five- or maybe a ten-year-old. Also, some may lack adequate small-muscle co-ordination to perform thorough plaque-control procedures for themselves.

Some of the techniques that work well with children are applicable here. If the individual **has control of facial muscles and is reasonably co-operative**, try using the following suggestions:

▶ **When performing oral hygiene procedures for a dependent person, always keep your fingers in positions that you cannot be bitten.**

▶ Encourage independent brushing once a day under casual supervision.

▶ Maintain the habit of thorough plaque removal once a day by a caregiver.

▶ Use disposable flossers or other interproximal cleaning aids as appropriate (please see *Chapter 12* for specific information on these devices).

▶ Clean the most critical interproximal areas first while co-operation is at its best.

▶ Use a soft brush with small head in a gentle scrub manner concentrating on the areas of the teeth closest to the gums. If tolerated, an electric toothbrush will disturb more plaque in a shorter time than manual brushing.

▶ Do the most **inaccessible** areas (where plaque likes to accumulate most heavily) first: the tongue side of the lower teeth and the cheek sides of the upper teeth.

▶ Use only a "pea-sized" amount of toothpaste on the brush. Choose a paste containing fluoride if it is appropriate (see guidelines on use of fluoride in *Chapter 9*).

▶ If the individual can rinse and spit out, ask your dentist if use of an OTC (over-the-counter, i.e. non-prescription) mouthwash with fluoride is appropriate. If approved, use only as directed.

▶ To establish the helping relationship, do oral hygiene care **every day**. Always work within the level of co-operation offered and praise positive behaviours. Never let oral hygiene assistance become a contest of wills.

Persons Lacking Muscle Control

Lack of muscle control can manifest in three basic forms:

▶ spastic movements which occur spontaneously and with considerable force (e.g. cerebral palsy)

▶ general lack of muscle tone where the mouth may be open much of the time (e.g. muscular dystrophy, Down's syndrome)

▶ lack of muscle tone which makes it difficult to keep the mouth open for more than a few seconds at a time.

Individuals with spastic muscles or general lack of muscle tone who have normal behavioural and social responses may be able to perform some oral hygiene procedures independently. Adapting toothbrushes as described in *Chapter 12* may make brushing easier. Daily assistance to maintain adequate plaque control may still be necessary. The following suggestions may lead to better results:

▶ **When performing oral hygiene procedures for a dependent person, always keep your fingers in positions that you cannot be bitten.**

▶ Encourage independent brushing once a day under casual supervision. Adapt aids as appropriate.

▶ Ask your dentist about obtaining a professional rubber block mouth prop to use when providing assistance. These come in a variety of sizes. When placed between the biting surfaces of the back teeth, they support the jaw and prevent sudden closure of the mouth on a toothbrush or other aid. The hard rubber material absorbs the shock and protects the teeth from injury. Make sure that a string is attached through the small "eye" in the block. If during use, the block becomes dislodged and falls towards the throat, it can be retrieved easily. Place the block on one side of the arch while cleaning the opposite side. After use, rinse the block thoroughly. Sanitize it regularly by washing in the dishwasher or soaking it for a few minutes in very hot water.

▶ Maintain the habit of thorough plaque removal once a day by a caregiver.

▶ Use disposable flossers or other interproximal cleaning aids as appropriate (please see *Chapter 12* for specific information on these devices).

▶ Clean the most critical interproximal areas first while co-operation is at its best.

- Use a soft brush with small head in a gentle scrub manner concentrating on the areas of the teeth closest to the gums. If tolerated, an electric toothbrush will disturb more plaque in a shorter time than manual brushing.

- Do the most **inaccessible areas** (where plaque likes to accumulate most heavily) first: the tongue side of the lower teeth and the cheek sides of the upper teeth

- If the individual can rinse and spit out, use a pea-sized amount of toothpaste (containing fluoride if appropriate). If spitting is a problem, **use water or non-foaming, non-fluoride paste** that can be swallowed.

- Ask your dentist if use of an OTC mouthwash applied with a toothbrush or cotton swab is appropriate. If approved, use only as directed.

Persons in Semi-conscious or Comatose States

These individuals are completely dependent on a personal care assistant for mouth hygiene. Usually persons in this state do not display strong spastic muscle contractions unless they suffer a seizure. They may, however, display some muscle and tongue movement in response to stimulation.

Even many professional personal care workers find providing adequate oral care difficult for these clients. The following suggestions may make this task easier:

- **When performing oral hygiene procedures for a dependent person, always keep your fingers in positions that you cannot be bitten.**

- Use of a mouth prop will make oral hygiene procedures easier to perform. If the person's facial muscles are usually quite slack, a useful mouth prop can be made of a standard wooden tongue depressor. Unfold a 2" x 2" gauze square and wrap it snuggly around one end of the tongue depressor to form a cushion. Open the mouth carefully and insert the mouth prop with the edges contacting the biting surfaces of the upper and lower back teeth on one side of the arch. This will support the mouth open wide enough to perform hygiene procedures on the opposite side of the arch. Change sides and continue. Dispose of the mouth prop when finished. If muscle resistance is strong enough that a single tongue depressor may be likely to break, tape two together for added strength.

- Ideally, thorough plaque removal should be done by a caregiver every day. If interproximal cleaning is very difficult, even once or twice a week is better than not at all.

▶ Use disposable flossers or other interproximal cleaning aids as appropriate (please see *Chapter 12* for specific information on these devices).

▶ Clean the most critical interproximal areas first.

▶ Use a soft brush with small head in a gentle scrub manner concentrating on the areas of the teeth closest to the gums. If tolerated, an electric toothbrush will disturb more plaque in a shorter time than manual brushing.

▶ Do the most **inaccessible areas** (where plaque likes to accumulate most heavily) first: the tongue side of the lower teeth and the cheek sides of the upper teeth

▶ Use a wet brush or non-foaming, non-fluoride paste that can be swallowed.

▶ Ask your dentist if use of an OTC mouthwash applied with a toothbrush or cotton swab is appropriate. If approved, use only as directed.

Tooth Loss and Pregnancy: Myths Debunked

How often have women heard the axiom "one tooth lost for every child"? Many still believe tooth loss experienced around pregnancy resulted because "the baby robbed the calcium from my teeth." While it is certainly true some women experience tooth decay during pregnancy, it is not caused by the fetus. Once teeth calcify, there is no internal physiological process that will remove the minerals from them.

Some women may experience gum disease during pregnancy. In most cases, it is a result of hormone fluctuations and changing habits. Once the causes are understood, it is easy to adopt measures that reduce the risk.

Oral disease risk factors during pregnancy include:

▶ hormone changes resulting in morning sickness and "pregnancy gingivitis"

▶ changes in eating patterns and daily habits.

Morning Sickness

Facing morning is tough enough without having a bout of nausea and vomiting. Some women never have the inconvenience; some suffer for the usual three-month period and some even longer. Morning sickness poses a two-fold risk for tooth decay.

First, regurgitated stomach acid tends to settle around the teeth and on the tongue. It will demineralize tooth enamel even more readily than plaque acid. Second, when feeling nauseous, the last thing most people want to do is put something in their mouths. This combination of events results in poorer oral hygiene. Increased amounts of bacterial plaque, mixed with stomach acid create a potent attack on teeth.

Fight back by:

▶ rinsing your mouth after vomiting with lots of warm water to dilute the stomach acid. If you can stand the thought and the taste, dissolve about ½ tsp of ordinary baking soda in the water. It will help to neutralize the acid. **Do not brush your teeth to remove the acid**. While teeth are bathed in stomach acid they are much more susceptible to abrasion. Brushing at this point could do more harm than good.

▶ re-scheduling your major oral hygiene procedures to a time of day when your stomach is settled

▶ using toothpaste which contains fluoride will help to strengthen tooth enamel.

Pregnancy Gingivitis

If your mouth was clean and healthy before you got pregnant, you probably will not have pregnancy gingivitis. This problem usually occurs where oral hygiene and tissue health are poor to begin with. Changing hormone levels associated with pregnancy will make the existing disease worse.

Fight back by:

▶ visiting your dental professionals (preferably during the first trimester) to have your mouth examined and to have your teeth thoroughly cleaned

▶ faithfully following their recommendations for oral self care.

Changes in Eating Habits

Food cravings associated with pregnancy are grist for the joke and cartoon mills. If the list includes high-sugar foods such as hot fudge sundaes, chocolate cake, granola bars, etc., this could be a problem.

As the growing fetus impinges on mom's internal organs, many women are more comfortable eating several smaller meals per day. Food cravings and physiology may tempt women to eat many high-carbohydrate snacks every day. The increased frequency of sugar available to oral bacteria increases the length of time plaque acid can attack teeth and gums. For more details on oral disease processes please see *Chapter 8*.

Fight back by:

► keeping a supply of low-sugar, tasty, nutritious snack foods available (suggestions are listed in *Chapter 9*)

► indulging your cravings for sugar-rich foods only two or three times each day

► keeping oral plaque disrupted daily.

The rules for oral health during pregnancy are the same as pre-pregnancy habits:

► healthy eating patterns

► daily, thorough bacterial plaque disruption

► regular professional assistance.

If you don't let your new condition distract you from your healthy lifestyle, you should sail through pregnancy without dental problems.

Oral Self Care during Orthodontic Treatment

Wear and Care of Appliances

Very simply, your teeth will not move unless you wear your appliances as directed. If your appliances are removable, you may be able to develop a pattern of wearing them or not that will fool your parents but not your orthodontic team members. They will note there has been little progress in your treatment. If your appliances are attached to your teeth, they still need care to prevent breakage.

During orthodontic treatment oral hygiene is particularly important. Tissues are already under strain from tooth movement. They should not be doubly assaulted by the presence of disease-producing plaque. Fixed appliances make oral hygiene maintenance more difficult but with a bit of extra time and care this can be done well each day. Table 11.1 later in this chapter summarizes the wear and care information for several kinds of orthodontic appliances.

Soft Tissue Changes

During orthodontic treatment the soft tissues of the mouth change, especially the free gingiva. Although tooth movement is relatively slow, it occurs more rapidly than the re-sculpting of the gingival tissues. Gum tissue appears puffy and bulky as it tends to "pile up" in response to tooth movement. Poor oral hygiene will make the situation worse because unhealthy tissue has a tendency to swell and make the tissue mass even larger. You can help control the tissue enlargement by regular, gentle massage of the affected areas using a soft toothbrush or a clean finger. The massage promotes blood flow in the area which increases the cellular activity towards removal of the excess tissue.

When tooth movement is complete and retaining appliances are placed, normal tissue contours will be re-established around the teeth in their new positions.

Oral Self Care

During active orthodontic therapy you should try to brush after eating. This action will keep ugly food debris off your appliances as well as help to control the development of dental plaque.

Thorough plaque removal once ever 24 hours is still the standard required to maintain oral health. Within reason, be creative about your oral hygiene practices during treatment. The constraints are:

▶ **Do not** damage soft tissue or appliances while removing plaque.

▶ Brush after eating to remove food debris.

▶ Rinse thoroughly with water when brushing is not possible.

▶ Use soft brushes with small heads: a number of styles (standard, powered, end tuft, interproximal brush, etc.) used in sequence may provide the best results. For illustrations of specialty brushes and other interproximal cleaning aids that may be helpful, please see *Chapter 12*.

▶ Concentrate the majority of brushing time on the gums and the area of the tooth between the bracket and arch wires and the gums. This is where the plaque tends to collect. If left undisturbed it can cause permanent white marks on your teeth and eventually cavities.

▶ Brush first using water only (it is easier to assess results), then use a small amount of toothpaste containing fluoride to help strengthen enamel.

▶ Use a fluoride mouthrinse as directed, if your dentist or orthodontist recommends it. Remember, using fluoride is not a substitute for excellent oral hygiene.

▶ If you hadn't learned to floss before your appliances were placed, postpone mastering that skill until your fixed appliances are removed.

▶ If you were in the habit of using floss, you can still do so using a threader (please see *Chapter 12,* figure 12.4) to carry the floss under the arch wires. You may find flossing once a day is more time-consuming than you can manage, but doing it as often as possible will be helpful.

Dietary Considerations

Factors to remember:

▶ With oral plaque control more difficult, teeth and soft tissues are more susceptible to disease.

▶ Cellular changes in the tissues require adequate nutrients for best results.

▶ Fixed intra-oral appliances can be broken.

▶ Post-operative discomfort occurs after appliance adjustments.

Therefore try to follow these recommendations:

▶ Eat a well balanced diet every day.

▶ Use multivitamin supplements if your practitioners advise.

▶ Restrict the frequency of starchy and sugary food to three times per day.

▶ Avoid chewing gum, sticky toffee and other foods which damage appliances.

▶ Cut hard foods such as raw carrots, apples, celery, etc., into bite-sized pieces or thin sticks to avoid damaging arch wires or dislodging bonded brackets when biting.

▶ During post-operative discomfort phase choose nutritious foods which are easy to eat e.g. soups, milkshakes blended with fresh fruits, eggnogs, etc.

Post-operative Discomfort

When appliances are first placed and after adjustments expect some post-operative discomfort. The soft tissue of the lips and cheeks take some time to adjust. Use a small piece of wax (supplied by your orthodontist) for a day or two to cover any part of the appliance which may be irritating the soft tissue. Don't overuse wax because it only delays adaptation of the tissues to the appliances.

Discomfort after an appliance adjustment occurs as tenderness when chewing or sometimes a dull, continuous ache or occasionally a headache. This discomfort usually disappears in 24-48 hours. Try the following to help you through this phase:

▶   Eat nutritious soft foods.

▶   Rinse with warm saline solution (½ tsp or 2.5 ml table salt in a juice-sized glass of water) several times a day, for about one minute each time. This tends to reduce swelling in the soft tissue.

▶   Massage the tender areas gently with a soft toothbrush or clean finger to increase blood flow.

▶   Take the recommended dose of a mild analgesic if required (ASA, ibuprofen, etc.)

If the discomfort is severe, lasts beyond the 48-hour time frame, or is not helped by these actions, contact your orthodontist for further advice.

Appliance Breakage

Even with careful attention, accidents can happen and appliances can get broken. If breakage occurs within 72 hours of a regularly scheduled appointment, an emergency visit can usually be prevented if:

▶   the damaged piece of the appliance can be removed easily

▶   the damaged area can be successfully covered with wax to protect soft tissue

▶   the bonded bracket or band has loosened but is still attached to the arch wire.

If you are in doubt about taking any of these actions call the orthodontist for advice. The damaged part of the appliance should be taken to the office if possible. If your next scheduled visit is more than three days away, the office should be notified and a suitable appointment time arranged.

If a removable appliance (intra-oral or head gear) is damaged or deformed making it difficult to insert, do not attempt to adjust it or force it into place. An office visit (as described earlier) is the appropriate action.

Table 11.1 Wear and Care of Orthodontic Appliances		
Appliance	Wear	Care
Intra-oral functional or Hawley type with active components	► worn 24 hours per day ► removed only for meals and cleaning	► cleaned with a soft toothbrush and water (with or without low-abrasive toothpaste) before insertion into the mouth ► appliance taken to all office visits for adjustment
Hawley type retainers	► worn 24 hours per day for the first 6-12 months post-treatment, and nights for the next 6-12 months ► can be worn during meals if desired	► cleaned with a soft toothbrush and water (with or without low- abrasive toothpaste) after meals ► stored in water when not in the mouth ► appliance taken to all office visits for adjustment
Extra-oral traction appliances	► worn as much as possible ► usually 12-14 hours per day minimum (evenings and during sleep) ► most practitioners do not expect clients to wear these appliances in public places	► intra-oral components cleaned with a soft toothbrush and water (with or without low-abrasive toothpaste) before insertion into the mouth ► extra-oral straps washed in warm soapy water as required ► appliance taken to all office visits for adjustment
Removable components of fixed appliances (e.g. intra-oral elastics)	► worn 24 hours per day ► removed only for meals and for oral hygiene practices ► elastics replaced if broken ► elastics replaced at least every 24 hours or as directed by practitioner	► always have spare elastics available

Occasionally, even with regular care, hard deposits can build up on intra-oral removable appliances. These can usually be removed by soaking the appliance in a solution of equal parts white vinegar and water for 12-24 hours. This typically softens the deposits so they can be removed with a soft toothbrush.

Denture Care

The materials used to make partial and complete dentures are similar to those used in removable orthodontic appliances. It is not surprising, then, that the care of dentures is similar to care of appliances already described.

Dentures should be removed and cleaned after eating to ensure food particles are not trapped on visible surfaces or between the denture base and soft tissue. A simple rinse under the tap may be all that is required. Use of water and a soft toothbrush is also helpful.

Oral tissues remain healthy when exposed to normal stimulation during eating. When partial or complete dentures cover oral tissues, this stimulation is not present. Also, the tissue is under the stress of supporting the denture. It is important to remove dentures while sleeping to give these tissues a rest and provide them with normal exposure to tongue movements and saliva flow.

Before bedtime, brush any food debris or soft deposits from your dentures with water and a soft brush. Use a denture soaking solution to store them overnight. This will help remove stains and odours.

Even with careful attention, hard deposits can build up on dentures in some areas. When this happens, switch the overnight soaking solution to a solution mixed with equal parts of plain white vinegar and water for a few nights. This will not hurt the denture material and will eventually soften the calcified deposits so they can be removed with a soft brush.

Maintaining Your Motivation

Dental disease is closely connected to lifestyle. As you know, many healthy lifestyle choices can get to be a bit of a drag. Sticking to a sound oral care program can feel that way too, especially at first as you are struggling to perfect new plaque-control routines.

Remember, most worthwhile things in life require a little effort. The following hints may make it easier for you to adopt and stick to a healthy routine.

► If your oral care habits require a lot of change, start with the easiest aspect to master, then move on to the more difficult activities.

► Choose a time to begin learning new skills when other aspects of your life are going well. This will reduce the frustration of coping with a new routine.

▶ Make sure that you have time to practise your new plaque-control skill well each day. As you become more proficient, the time required to do a thorough job will decrease.

▶ Make a pact with yourself to be diligent and work at the new routine every day for at least four weeks. It takes about that long for most people to see the routine as a habit worth maintaining.

▶ Be patient with yourself. Some of the new plaque-control devices and methods of using them are tricky. Practice really does make perfect.

▶ Try to piggy-back plaque control with another daily activity (watching the news, reading the paper, etc.) That way you won't feel you are "wasting" time doing your oral plaque control.

▶ Look for the following rewards to better oral cleanliness in the short term:

> cleaner-feeling teeth
> fresher-tasting mouth
> fresher breath
> no bleeding gums

▶ Look forward to the following benefits over the long haul:

> easier professional cleaning appointments
> fewer or no cavities
> lower dental bills.

Regular Professional Assistance

The most important key to a healthy mouth is the lifestyle of its owner. Even the most zealous oral health "nut" will require professional assistance on a regular basis. There will always be pesky areas around teeth and gums that cannot be maintained deposit free through home care alone.

Regular health assessments and dental cleanings performed by professionals need to be part of your overall strategy for maintaining oral health. Frequency of dental visits varies from one individual to another. Your dental professional will advise you on what interval suits your particular needs.

Bruxism (teeth-grinding habit)

Not all people who grind their teeth are aware they have the habit. It usually occurs when sleeping or unconsciously during the day. A sleep partner kept awake by the gnashing can attest to the habit. Co-workers nearby may also know about a person's grinding habit. Members of the dental team may spot the excessive wear to the biting surfaces which is the hallmark of bruxism.

In addition to annoying others, bruxism is not healthy for the one doing the grinding. As already mentioned, the habit can cause unusual or extensive wear to the tooth surfaces involved. The unnatural forces exerted on the dentition can also cause trauma to the periodontal tissues which support the teeth. Many grinders also experience tooth tenderness, facial muscle stiffness or discomfort and eventually pain and dysfunction in the jaw joint.

Numerous theories abound regarding causes. Stress is the culprit usually blamed but there is no hard evidence to identify causes reliably. Since causes are speculative, treatment options address protection of the oral tissues at risk.

The most common treatment for bruxism is fabrication of an appliance known as a bite plane or nightguard. This is an acrylic device which fits over the biting surfaces of the teeth in one arch (usually the lower). It is made by taking an impression of the arch, pouring a model and molding the material along the biting surface and down the sides of the teeth about one third of their length. The imprint of the teeth fits over the arch and holds the appliance in place.

The name bite plane comes from the fact that the surface facing the opposing teeth in the other arch is smooth. When the teeth come in contact with the smooth acrylic surface of the bite plane they tend to slide across it. This reduces the stress on the periodontal tissues, facial muscles and jaw joint. The appliance also prevents more wear to the biting surfaces of the teeth.

Clients with grinding habits can be fitted for a bite plane by their family dentist. If they are experiencing symptoms of discomfort in teeth, muscles or joints, they will probably be advised to wear the appliance 24 hours a day for a few weeks or a few months. At first the appliance may cause some difficulty with speech but it is usually temporary. When the symptoms subside, the appliance can be used only when sleeping. If the symptoms do not subside, further investigation of their causes is indicated.

Wear and Care of a Bite Plane

If you are advised to wear the appliance 24 hours per day you are permitted to remove it to eat. It should be cleaned with a soft brush and rinsed before being placed back in your mouth. Daily cleaning with a good denture cleaner is also appropriate.

If you are wearing it part-time, it should be stored in water (or denture-cleaning solution). If you see hard deposits anywhere on the appliance don't try to scrape them off with a metal device. Mix a solution of white vinegar and water (about half and half) and soak the appliance for several hours until the deposits are soft enough to brush off.

If the appliance becomes visibly damaged or if it is difficult to insert or remove, have it checked by your dental practitioner.

Tooth Safety

With obesity rates, especially in children, climbing annually, everyone is encouraged to become more physically active. Many activities and sports may pose a risk to the dentition. Proper protective gear is important. For those playing contact sports, such as football, hockey and various kinds of self defense activities, a custom-fitted mouthguard should be worn when participating.

"One-size-fits-all" mouthguards which are available will not offer optimal protection. Home "custom" mouthguard kits can be purchased in many sports equipment stores and pharmacies. They are only marginally better. Home-fitted guards are often too flimsy to be effective. They may fit so poorly they can become dislodged and injure soft tissue in the mouth during wear.

The best protection is provided by a professionally fitted custom mouthguard. To make one, an impression is taken of the upper arch and a model poured and trimmed. A sheet of sturdy plastic material is heated until it is very pliable and then fitted snuggly to the model using a vacuum device. The material is then cooled and the guard trimmed so that it covers the teeth without impinging on gum tissue. The trimmed edges will be smoothed for comfort to cheeks and lips. The client will try the guard and it will be adjusted as necessary for fit and comfort.

In most organized sports leagues at all levels, appropriate protective equipment is mandatory for all scheduled practices and games. Participants are sidelined if they do not comply. Neighbourhood pick-up games can be just as dangerous to the dentition. Make sure to wear protective gear during all risky sports activities.

Mouthguard Care

When not being worn, guards should be stored in a clean carrying case. The guard should be rinsed when removed from the mouth and placed in the case. At home, the guard and case should be cleaned thoroughly. A toothbrush and water or some mouthwash will freshen both. Rinse and dry the guard and case before storing for next use.

Chapter 12
Adaptive Oral Hygiene Aids

In This Chapter

▶ modified toothbrushes
▶ specialty toothbrushes
▶ powered toothbrushes
▶ interproximal cleaning devices
▶ oral irrigation devices

Modified Toothbrushes

Chapters 10 and 11 provided information on mechanical oral plaque control for people of all ages. This chapter is for those who find ordinary toothbrushes and dental floss are not the answer. Some possible modifications to standard toothbrushes that might be helpful are discussed here.

If you have difficulty grasping a standard toothbrush, try enlarging the handle. A Styrofoam ball (available at most craft stores) can be hollowed out to accept the handle. These balls are lightweight, fairly hardy and come in a variety of sizes. They are inexpensive enough to replace as frequently as necessary. Choose a size that is most comfortable for your particular grip and place it on the brush handle in the position that suits you best. A tennis ball may also be used to enlarge the handle of the brush but is more difficult to puncture. A toothbrush handle can also be enlarged by inserting it into a plastic bicycle handlebar grip.

A strap can be attached to a standard toothbrush handle to make the brush more stable in the hand during use. Pieces of Velcro are placed at right angles to the handle so that the ends can close over the back of the hand to support the grip on the brush.

If you have difficulty raising your arm to your mouth and holding it there long enough to do a thorough brushing job, try lengthening the brush handle. One of the following taped to the handle might do the trick:

▶ a sturdy ruler
▶ a short dowel with a diameter which is comfortable for your grasp
▶ several tongue depressors, taped together

Specialty Toothbrushes

A variety of small-headed toothbrushes is available. These are designed to clean areas that are difficult to reach with conventional brushes. They can be particularly useful for individuals who have lost some periodontal tissue or who are having fixed-appliance orthodontic treatment.

Some popular styles of these brushes are shown in figure 12.1.

Fig. 12.1. Small-headed toothbrushes showing bristle profiles.

Powered Toothbrushes

A large variety of powered toothbrushes is now available. Most consist of an enlarged handle that contains the power pack and removable brush heads. Brush heads are replaced when worn and come in several colours allowing numerous members in the family to use the same powered handle. Some types of power packs are recharged by setting them in a stand which is connected to a standard electrical outlet. Other powered brushes use standard batteries which are replaced when depleted.

The size and shape of the brush heads are specific to the manufacturer. Some are shaped like a standard toothbrush; some are circular. Each design has a specific programmed motion to the brush head while in operation. All powered brushes have some advantages and disadvantages.

Advantages include:

▶ Built-in tiny vibrating, pulsing or circular motion of the brush head. This means the user simply needs to place and guide the brush to reach all areas of the mouth.

▶ Enlarged handles that some people may find easier to grasp.

▶ Longer handles which may provide help for those with difficulty holding their arms up long enough to brush thoroughly.

▶ A timer to indicate when appropriate brushing time is up.

Disadvantages:

▶ Most powered brushes are considerably heavier than manual brushes.

▶ Powered brushes may encourage you to spend too little time on brushing – not long enough to do a thorough job.

▶ Some people find the rapid movement of the brush head is initially annoying. The sensation may take some getting used to.

▶ Powered brushes are considerably more expensive than manual brushes, not only at initial purchase, but also for replacement brush heads and, if applicable, batteries.

If you are contemplating purchase of a powered brush, discuss your intentions with your oral care practitioner. S/he can offer suggestions regarding the type best suited to your needs. Some dental offices keep a variety of powered brushes on hand which you may examine and perhaps try out, in order to choose one most helpful to you.

If you have already purchased a powered brush and find it less helpful than you bargained for, take it to your next dental appointment and ask your practitioner for advice on using it for optimal benefit.

Interproximal Cleaning Devices

To Floss …

If using your fingers to floss leaves you all thumbs, try using a floss holder as illustrated in figure 12.2. Place the floss in the slots in the 'fingers" of the holder and secure the ends around the wheel. Guide the floss in a back and forth motion between the teeth. Press against the side of one tooth at a time and sweep the floss towards the biting surface. Clean the adjacent tooth in the same manner before removing it through the contact area. Proceed around the arch until all proximal surfaces have been cleaned. Don't forget to change the floss between the arms of the holder each time you move to a new area of the mouth.

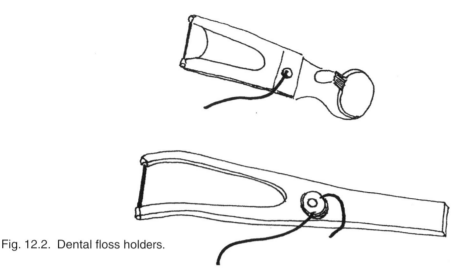

Fig. 12.2. Dental floss holders.

Small, single-use flossing devices are also available (figure 12.3). They are another alternative to standard flossing techniques. They can be particularly useful when flossing for children or others who need assistance with oral hygiene procedures.

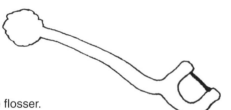

Fig. 12.3. Disposable flosser.

For individuals with fixed bridgework or fixed orthodontic appliances, the bridge or the arch wires will block access of floss between the teeth. Flossing can still be accomplished by using one of a variety of flexible plastic floss-threading devices. Tie a piece of floss to the eye of the floss threader (see figure 12.4) and use the device to carry the floss under the bridge or arch wire. The teeth in that area can now be flossed in the normal manner.

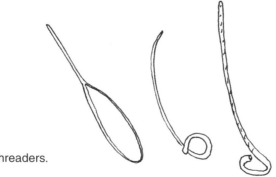

Fig. 12.4. Floss threaders.

Since fixed bridgework usually affects only a few teeth, flossing in this manner is advised and not too time-consuming once the technique is mastered.

For individuals with full-mouth fixed orthodontic appliances, this method works but is time-consuming. Adequate interproximal cleaning usually can be accomplished with less frustration using other tools.

Powered floss devices are also available. Discuss these with your dental professional to see if they are advisable for your needs.

... Or Not To Floss

If you have given dental floss your best effort and it still isn't for you, take heart. There are options for interproximal cleaning. Read the information below and decide which device might suit you best.

Interproximal Toothbrushes

The mini-toothbrush (see figure 12.5A) fits between teeth, below their points of contact. It is designed to clean the surfaces below the gum line where normal brushes won't reach. Use the device by directing the point of the brush head at right angles to the teeth. Insert the tip carefully between adjacent teeth, below the contact point between them. Coax it in beside the soft tissue in the space. Be careful not to damage the gums. Work the brush with a gentle push and pull motion to disturb the plaque.

Start from the facial side of the arch. Begin at one back end of the arch and work around to the opposite end. Work your way back around the same arch, this time inserting the brush into each space from the tongue side of the teeth. **Use the brush only in areas where it fits comfortably.** If your teeth are crowded or some of them are rotated, there may be areas that the brush can't access. You may still need to floss a few places.

Interproximal brush heads come in two basic shapes: tapered and cylindrical (figures 12.5B and12.5C). A number of sizes are available. Fine brushes are more suitable for individuals with normal bone heights around each tooth. If you have experienced periodontal disease which resulted in bone loss, a larger circumference brush tip will be more helpful to you. Many of the handles (figure 12.5B) used with these brushes are double-ended. Placing brushes of different designs in each end will allow you to have the right shape and size of brush ready to accommodate all interproximal spaces around the arch. You will soon learn which end fits where.

Brush heads need to be replaced frequently. No need to buy a new handle each time as packages of replacement brushes are sold separately.

Fig. 12.5A. Interproximal toothbrush.

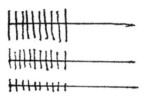

Fig. 12.5B. Handle with replaceable interproximal brush.

Fig. 12.5C. Sizes and styles of brush replacements.

Wedge-shaped Toothpicks

These specially designed toothpicks can help remove impacted food and disturb plaque between teeth. They are made of wood which becomes slightly softened in saliva. In cross section they are triangular in shape.

Use of a wedge-shaped toothpick is similar to the motion of the interproximal toothbrush described above. Make sure the flat side of the wedge is towards the gum tissue. Aim the point at right angles to the teeth. Slide the pick gently between the teeth, under their point of contact. Be careful not to injure the gums. Slide the toothpick in and out of the space to remove food and disturb plaque in the area. Work your way around the arches in a systematic manner. The biggest disadvantage of this device is the inability of most people to use it from the tongue side of the teeth. Use the toothpick only where space and tooth position allows easy access.

Fig. 12.6A. Wedge-shaped toothpick.

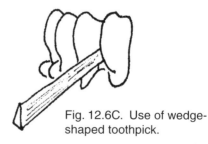

Fig. 12.6C. Use of wedge-shaped toothpick.

Fig. 12.6B. Cross-section of wedge-shaped toothpick.

Soft Toothpicks

Packages of cone-shaped toothpicks made of flexible plastic are now available. They have a flat handle which makes them quite easy to manipulate. These can be used in the same manner as the interproximal toothbrush and the wedge-shaped toothpick described earlier.

Other Plaque-disturbing Aids

Single-tufted Toothbrushes

These double-ended brushes sport very small, relatively stiff brushing heads on each end of a specifically angled handle. Each brush has a pointed end which helps reach between teeth and slightly below the gum line.

These brushes are helpful in areas where gum recession makes cleaning along the gum line a challenge. Running the tip of the brush lightly along the gum line helps to disrupt plaque which accumulates there. Using them at right angles between the teeth below the contact will access a portion of the interproximal surfaces but will not do the whole job.

As with any device, for best results, it needs to be used for the purpose intended. Use light pressure to avoid damaging soft tissue. Single-tufted brushes are meant to be used in addition to regular brushing practices, not as replacements.

Chemical Plaque Control

Although chemical plaque control has serious drawbacks (for more information please see *Chapter 10*), some people can derive significant benefit from use of such agents. Typically they are supplied for home use as mouthrinses. There is a variety of therapeutic (disease-reducing) formulations available. Your dental practitioner will advise you on whether or not regular use of such an agent is appropriate.

Generally, therapeutic mouthrinses are considered advantageous under the following circumstances:

► where self-care procedures have failed to achieve adequate plaque control using other means

► where oral hygiene is difficult to maintain for individuals who are physically or developmentally challenged

► where maintenance of tissue health around dental implants is necessary.

All mouthrinses will act only on the bacteria living superficially on oral tissues. They will not flow below the gum tissue (free gingiva).

Oral Irrigation Devices

As the name implies, oral irrigation involves the use of fluids under pressure to help clean the mouth. A variety of devices and fluids may be indicated for use. Oral irrigation procedures may be used by your dental practitioner to target localized sites of persistent periodontal disease. You may be shown how to perform oral irrigation in your own mouth to help maintain health in specific areas. For more information on this topic, please see *Chapter 4*.

Fluids used for oral irrigation can be water or solutions of antimicrobial agents designed to control bacterial growth. Devices vary from simple hand-held syringes through commercially available pressure syringe-like units attached to taps or self-contained reservoirs in which the fluid of choice is placed.

It is important to realize what oral irrigation can and cannot accomplish.

Oral irrigation **can**:

▶ help flush food debris from superficial tooth surfaces (this may be helpful during orthodontic treatment with fixed appliances in place)

▶ direct fluids below the gums into periodontal pockets (useful for short-term delivery of antimicrobial agents to specific sites in the treatment of periodontal disease)

▶ **cause significant damage to periodontal tissues if powered commercial units are used incorrectly at high-pressure settings.**

Oral irrigation **cannot**:

▶ mechanically disrupt organized bacterial plaque anywhere in the mouth at any pressure setting.

Ask your dental practitioner if and how oral irrigation should be added to your self-care routine. To be sure you are gaining benefit and reducing the risk of harm, you should practise the techniques recommended under the watchful eye of your practitioner until you are proficient.

Chapter 13

Mouth Care and Medical Complications

In This Chapter

- ▶ heart disease
- ▶ total joint replacement (prosthesis)
- ▶ diabetes mellitus
- ▶ radiation therapy of the head and neck
- ▶ chemotherapy for cancer
- ▶ hiv and aids
- ▶ reduced immune system function

Although the eyes may be the windows to the soul, the mouth can indicate a great deal about the overall health of its owner. Some systemic diseases have oral manifestations. Treatment protocols for some serious illnesses can also cause oral problems. Basic information about some of these associations among common diseases, their treatments and oral implications are described in this chapter.

Individuals experiencing any of these conditions should discuss appropriate individualized treatment with the medical and dental professionals managing their care.

Heart Disease

For individuals with a history of heart disease, maintaining excellent oral hygiene by using effective daily home-care procedures is particularly important. Please see *Chapters 11* and *12* for detailed information on self-care strategies. Regular professional care is also a must.

When soft mouth tissues are not healthy, they tend to bleed. If blood can leak out, bacteria can leak in. Once in the bloodstream, bacteria circulate throughout the body. If the bacterial load is high enough, serious heart infections called infective endocarditis can occur.

Routine scaling and root-planing techniques and other dental procedures usually cause some bleeding. To prevent endocarditis the dentist will prescribe antibiotics to be taken before and after treatment appointments.

Types of heart conditions where antibiotic coverage is necessary for dental treatment include:

▶   congenital heart disease (unrepaired; repaired with residual defects; completely repaired, within the first six months after repair procedure)

▶   prosthetic heart valves

▶   history of infective endocarditis

▶   heart transplant recipients who develop heart valve pathology.

Clients with heart problems must give their dental practitioners details of their cardiac disease history. The dentist can then accurately determine risks for treatment and provide pre- and post-appointment care with appropriately chosen antibiotics.

Total Joint Replacement (Prosthesis)

Clients with certain bone disease histories may also require antibiotics prior to dental treatment. The rationale for coverage is the same as that described for heart disease earlier in this chapter. If bleeding is initiated by dental treatment, the bacteria from the mouth can circulate through the bloodstream into joint regions. An infection may damage the tissue around an unrepaired diseased joint, or a prosthesis, and put the joint at risk. Antibiotics are indicated under the following circumstances:

▶   within the first two years after prosthetic joint-replacement surgery

▶   when inflammatory bone disease is present, e.g. rheumatoid arthritis, systemic lupus erythematosus

▶   for clients who have histories of prosthetic joint infection

▶   for clients who are malnourished

▶   for clients who also have hemophilia

▶   for clients with type 1 (insulin-dependent) diabetes

▶ for clients with malignancies

▶ for clients with suppressed immune system function due to HIV infection, radiation therapy or drug therapy.

Diabetes Mellitus

The incidence of diabetes in the developed world is on the rise. Initial symptoms are often subtle and many people who have the disease are unaware of it. Although at the moment there is no cure for diabetes, once diagnosed it can be controlled effectively. Living with controlled diabetes over time increases the risk for developing other health challenges. These include: damage to eyes, kidneys and skin as well as damage to the circulatory, reproductive and nervous systems.

Diabetes is also a significant risk for periodontal disease. The diabetes-periodontal disease relationship is a two-way interaction. Poorly controlled diabetes increases the risk for periodontal disease and once tissues are diseased, blood glucose levels become harder to control. This interdependent relationship makes maintaining oral health an important aspect of coping with diabetes. Tissue healing is delayed when diabetes is present, so prevention of oral disease is doubly important. Home-care strategies are described in detail in *Chapters 11 and 12*.

Regular professional care is also necessary to support home oral hygiene efforts. The dental team may prefer to schedule appointments every three or four months. With this recall frequency, deposit build-up should be minimal and dental visits shorter and less stressful.

Individuals who have any of the following signs and symptoms should have their family doctor check them for diabetes. As a reminder, the signs of diabetes include:

▶ frequent dry mouth and excessive thirst

▶ frequent bathroom visits (more than six per day) to urinate (pass water)

▶ unexplained and unplanned weight loss.

If there is a history of diabetes in the family, the risk of becoming diabetic increases. Other risk factors include increasing age, obesity, poor diet and lack of exercise.

Radiation Therapy of the Head and Neck

When cancerous tumours are diagnosed in the region of the head and neck, treatment usually consists of some combination of surgery, radiation and chemotherapy. When radiation is used, the side effects depend on the site of exposure and the dose administered.

Side effects are usually noticeable by the end of the first week of treatment. They can be described as acute (those that persist during the course of treatment but dissipate when treatment is finished) and chronic (those effects that persist even after treatment is ended).

Acute side effects may include:

▶ change in saliva composition to thick and "ropey"

▶ dry mouth

▶ reduction in taste (if the tongue is irradiated)

▶ soft tissue irritation and risk of secondary infection causing pain and difficulty eating

▶ difficulty swallowing

▶ reduced ability to open the mouth if the muscles controlling chewing are exposed to radiation

▶ hearing loss

▶ fatigue

▶ reduced nutrition due to dry mouth, poor taste and difficulty swallowing.

Chronic side effects may include:

▶ salivary gland impairment leading to persistent dry mouth

▶ alteration in taste

▶ increased susceptibility to oral infections

► soft tissue and bone degeneration

► severe dental decay

► jaw joint dysfunction and limited mouth opening due to muscle damage.

For children undergoing cancer therapy of the head and neck, development of the teeth and jaws may be altered.

Table 13.1 contains suggestions for coping with the side effects of radiation therapy.

Table 13.1 Coping with Side Effects of Radiation Therapy for Cancers of the Head and Neck	
Side Effect	Commonly Used Coping Strategies
dry mouth	► sip water, suck ice chips or hard sugarless candy, or chew sugarless gum ► use a prescribed or OTC saliva substitute ► avoid spicy foods and alcohol (including that in mouthwash) ► do not use tobacco (smoked or smokeless) ► moisturize lips with lip balm or cream (not petroleum jelly)
soft tissue irritation/ secondary infection	► keep mouth moist and maintain good oral hygiene ► use very soft toothbrushes and baking soda and water rather than flavoured toothpastes ► rinse frequently with salt and soda water mixed as follows: 5 ml (1 tsp) of soda and 2.5 ml (½ tsp) salt in 1 litre (32 oz) of water ► clean dentures well and remove overnight ► avoid spicy and rough-textured food ► use OTC analgesics for pain
muscle impairment/jaw joint dysfunction	► prevent long-term disability by exercising 3 times per day by opening the mouth as wide as possible without pain and closing it again ► do 20 repetitions of the exercise
tooth decay (radiation induced) within the first year post radiation	► maintain excellent mechanical plaque removal (please see *Chapters 10 and 11*) ► use fluoride gel in a professionally custom-fitted tray as prescribed by the dentist (usually daily) when radiation treatment begins; continue as directed ► if tissue irritation occurs, replace tray-applied fluoride with bland fluoride mouthwash with a lower concentration until irritation subsides ► avoid foods and beverages high in sugar and acids (including soda pops with artificial sweeteners)
soft tissue and bone degeneration	► radiation injury to the blood supply may cause irreversible changes resulting in long-term reduction in healing potential of tissues ► tissues are less resistant to infection
hearing loss and fatigue	► hearing loss and physical energy usually return sometime after treatment is completed ► during treatment, rest as required

Chemotherapy for Cancer

Many treatment protocols for various types of cancer include drug therapy to destroy cancer cells or to reduce the risk of recurrence of the disease. Potential side effects of these medications include: reduced immune system function, bleeding, nausea, increased sensitivity to light and hair loss.

Not all chemotherapy agents cause oral effects. About 40 percent of people treated for cancers not located in the head and neck experience oral complications. Effects are usually not permanent but may occur throughout administration of the medication. The oncologist and dental team will provide specific information to each cancer patient about coping with the oral effects of treatment as they occur. The aim of dental care during cancer treatment is to have dental needs met before chemotherapy is initiated so that dental visits during the course of treatment are not required except in case of emergencies.

Table 13.2 describes potential oral complications and basic management strategies.

Table 13.2 Coping with Side Effects of Chemotherapy for Cancer	
Side Effect	Commonly Used Coping Strategies
soft tissue irritation (7-10 days after drug administration)	► keep mouth moist (sip water or suck ice chips, hard sugarless candy, or chew sugarless gum) ► maintain good oral hygiene ► rinse frequently with salt and soda water (see Table 13.1) ► eat a well balanced diet ► avoid spicy foods and alcohol (including that in mouthwash) ► do not use tobacco (smoked or smokeless) ► use systemic analgesics for discomfort
oral pain from nerve interference	► usually subsides within a few days of administration of the drug ► follow oncologist's recommended management advice
reduced immune system function	► increased risk of infection both orally and systemically as damaged oral tissues may provide access to the bloodstream for bacteria ► antibiotics may be prescribed prior to dental appointments to prevent systemic infection ► oral hygiene self-care procedures should be tailored to the individual and performed daily ► dental practitioners should monitor oral health maintenance frequently ► thorough denture cleaning is important ► dentures should be removed at night to rest tissues
salivary gland changes	► may or may not occur ► saliva may become thick and "ropey" ► the mouth may become dry ► use mouth hydration strategies described earlier in this table and in table 13.1

dental decay	▸ not directly caused by chemotherapy
	▸ usually results from reduced salivary flow and changes in diet to sugary and starchy foods that are easier to eat
	▸ eat a decay-preventing diet (please see *Chapter 9*)
	▸ maintain excellent oral hygiene
	▸ use fluoride applications as recommended by dental practitioners

HIV and AIDS

An individual may be infected with HIV (human immunodeficiency virus) without knowing it. It may be years before medical signs and symptoms of AIDS (acquired immunodeficiency disease) appear. A small percentage of people who test positive for the virus never develop full blown AIDS. HIV infection cannot be reversed and AIDS cannot be cured. Everyone needs to be responsible and take precautions to reduce the risk of getting the disease or passing it on.

Drugs to treat HIV infections were first developed in the 1980s. Advances have been made steadily since that time. Modern antiviral drugs used to treat AIDS significantly improve the quality and prolong the life of those infected. Table 13.3 provides basic information about common oral complications associated with AIDS.

Table 13.3 Common Oral Complications of AIDS	
Oral Effect	Description
lymphadenopathy	▸ swollen lymph glands in the neck
candidiasis	▸ fungal infection commonly called thrush
	▸ often seen in persons with AIDS
	▸ can also occur when HIV infection is not present
	▸ appears as smooth red patches on the tongue, palate or lining of the cheeks
angular chelitis	▸ red cracks or fissures at the corners of the mouth on the lips
	▸ can also occur when HIV infection is absent and the diet is poor (lacking in vitamins)
recurrent herpes simplex virus infections	▸ most people are exposed to herpes virus infections during their lifetime and can have recurrences which heal without complications
	▸ AIDS patients may have more frequent and severe recurrences that may lead to development of secondary infections by other bacteria or viruses
hairy leukoplakia	▸ thick, white, patchy lesions usually on the sides of the tongue
	▸ hairy leukoplakia is associated with infection with the Epstein-Barr virus
	▸ when seen it is a reliable indication that the individual is also infected with HIV or has AIDS
Kaposi's sarcoma	▸ a malignant tumour of soft oral tissue
	▸ appears as a flat reddish-blue or purple patch of any size
	▸ about 20 percent of people with AIDS will be affected by Kaposi's sarcomas
	▸ these sarcomas are usually treated by some combination of surgery, radiation and chemotherapy

oral warts	▶ caused by human papillomavirus
	▶ they can occur in people without HIV infections and are removable usually without recurrence
	▶ when HIV infection is present, they often recur after removal
periodontal disease: gingivitis and periodontitis	▶ for detailed information on causes and progression of periodontal disease please see *Chapter 8*
	▶ the incidence of periodontal disease is higher and the effects more severe when HIV infection is present
	▶ daily use of individualized oral self-care disease-prevention strategies is important for patients with AIDS
	▶ periodontal health maintenance appointments with dental practitioners should be more frequent to support home care efforts
	▶ pre-appointment antibiotic coverage may be recommended

Reduced Immune System Function

Other medical conditions may interfere with normal functioning of the immune system. Individuals for whom this occurs are at greater risk of developing the oral complications described in the previous table (table 13.3).

Additional factors reducing immune system efficiency include:

▶ diseases

▶ malnutrition

▶ drug therapy (for post-organ-transplant patients)

Advice from health care practitioners regarding wellness maintenance strategies should be followed carefully. Frequent professional assessment and supportive care are also important.

Part VI

A Pound of Cure

Chapter 14

Dental Restorations

In This Chapter

► restoration versus cure
► silver fillings (amalgam)
► gold restorations
► tooth-coloured fillings (composite resin)
► endodontics (the dreaded "root canal")
► tooth capping (crowns)
► dental bridges
► Maryland bridges
► dentures as a solution to dental problems
► removable partial dentures
► complete dentures
► overdentures
► implant-supported restorations

While to most people the term "dental restoration" may mean "fillings", in a broader sense it could range from replacing a small amount of tooth structure lost to decay or fracture to replacing all missing teeth with complete dentures. This wider range of topics will be examined in this chapter.

Restoration versus Cure

There is one very important thing to remember about restorations. They do **not cure** dental disease. A filling can only replace the portion of the tooth which has been damaged. The best restoration placed by the most competent dentist, using the finest materials available, is a poor substitute for normal healthy tooth tissues and structure. When a tooth has sustained damage by decay, fracture or severe wear, it may fail to function normally. The aim of restorative dentistry is to return tooth function. If a portion of a tooth has been broken off, or worn down, materials can be used to reproduce its natural shape and size.

If a tooth has been damaged by caries (tooth decay), the diseased portion of the tooth is removed and filling materials are placed into the cavity preparation to reproduce its normal shape. While this procedure temporarily halts the decay process in that part of the tooth, the disease will continue if conditions are favourable. For a complete discussion of the dental decay process please see *Chapter 8*.

Most people probably take dental fillings for granted. When a tooth needs repair they are confident it can be done so that it functions normally. Many hundreds of nameless people over the last 3,000 years have worked diligently to evolve the materials and techniques of restorative dentistry available today.

When people think about fillings three things are likely uppermost in their minds:

▶ Can I still chew on it?

▶ Will it look all right?

▶ What will it cost?

Following are details about three restorative materials: dental amalgam, gold and composite resin.

Silver Fillings (Amalgam)

First are the familiar "silver" fillings that are placed in back teeth. Although these restorations are usually so-called because of their colour, they do in fact contain a percentage of silver. The chemical name for them is dental amalgam. This metal alloy is a combination of silver, copper, tin and sometimes zinc, in solid particle form. These particles are then mixed with the liquid metal, mercury.

The addition of mercury to the alloy particles results in a pliable mass which can be condensed into the prepared tooth. The material undergoes chemical changes during the first few minutes after mixing which make it solid enough to be carved into the required shape. It takes about 24-48 hours for the material to reach its maximum compressive strength. During this time clients should be careful not to chew on the new restoration – particularly if it is large or complex. Most fractures of amalgam fillings occur in the first 24 hours after placement. On final set, a well placed amalgam restoration has approximately 75 to 90 percent of the compressive strength of healthy enamel tissue.

There is a relatively recent controversy about the use of mercury in dental fillings. Mercury has long been known as a toxic metal. If absorbed by the body in excessive amounts, it has well-documented adverse effects on the central nervous system. Monitoring of increased amounts of mercury in the environment has sparked renewed research into the safety of dental amalgam.

Modern technology has permitted the formulation of dental amalgam with extremely precise mercury/alloy ratios. This means that when the setting reaction is complete, there is a very tiny amount of free mercury available to be absorbed by the body.

The Canadian Dental Association, after extensive review of current research into the hazards posed by dental amalgam, has concluded that amalgam continues to be a safe and useful dental restorative material for most people. For those with known metal sensitivities to any of the components of dental amalgam alloy, it should not be used. Metal sensitive people should be treated with other materials.

Gold Restorations

For those who could afford it gold alloy was a popular restorative material during the early to mid-20th century. It is less frequently used today for average restorations. Well-fabricated gold fillings have the advantages of being highly serviceable and less susceptible to tarnish and corrosion than amalgam.

Gold, as a restorative material, has three major disadvantages:

- ► the cost of the material itself

- ► the necessity of being molten to assume the required shape. This means that extensive laboratory work is required to create the restoration outside the mouth. Laboratory fees plus additional chair time required to prepare the tooth and cement the final product in place add to the cost of the restorative service.

- ► the inability to adapt the colour to match tooth tissue.

Tooth-coloured Fillings (Composite Resin)

Human personalities have long favoured dental fillings which look like natural teeth. To satisfy this need, many formulations of materials which could be tinted to match normal tooth colours have been developed. The latest generation of aesthetic dental restorative material is called composite resin.

Until quite recently, many resin materials did not have the compressive strength to allow for their use in posterior teeth where the biting forces are the greatest. The formulations available now can be used to restore any surface of any tooth successfully.

Many people are requesting any restoration they require be done with resin materials. Some people are also having their amalgam restorations replaced with composite resins. Usually their motivation stems from two sources: fear of complications from amalgam and desire for the more pleasing appearance of the resin materials. Some dental practitioners have restricted their practices to the use of resin materials only and actively support client acceptance of these materials.

Many composite dental resins contain the compound "BIS-GMA", short for bisphenol-A glycidal methacrylate. This material is present in many other plastic materials as well. Currently there is some concern about ingestion of it as it tends to leach out of some plastic compounds. Research has not yet determined the validity of these concerns.

People who are allergy-free and in good health but are contemplating a move to make their mouths amalgam-free zones, should consider the information in table 14.1. It summarizes the advantages and disadvantages of restorative materials.

Table 14.1 Comparisons of Common Dental Restorative Materials		
Material	Advantages	Disadvantages
dental amalgam	▶ ease of manipulation (It requires the least operating time to insert and finish the restoration) ▶ relatively inexpensive ▶ may serve well for a decade or often considerably longer ▶ with wear can lose some marginal integrity with the tooth surface without causing recurrence of decay	▶ does not match tooth colour and is not used in teeth which are highly visible ▶ can become discoloured through tarnish and corrosion in mouth fluids ▶ some people have allergies to metal components in the alloy ▶ the procedure may cause some minor post-operative tooth sensitivity which usually dissipates in several days to a few weeks
composite resin	▶ can be shaded effectively to simulate tooth enamel ▶ products now available to restore both front and back teeth successfully ▶ can lose some marginal integrity with the tooth surface without causing recurrence of decay, but may cause increased tooth sensitivity	▶ is technique sensitive, i.e. slight variations in handling can affect the final result ▶ increased operating time increases cost ▶ depending on location, lifespan may be less than 10 years ▶ many people experience persistent or recurring post-operative tooth sensitivity ▶ may contain BIS-GMA

| cast gold alloy | ► can serve for 15-20 years
► material is highly resistant to tarnish and corrosion in mouth fluids | ► technically complex: dentist and lab technician must work well together for a good result
► material itself is expensive
► increased operating time increases cost
► does not match tooth colour
► some people have allergies to metal components in the alloy
► procedure may cause some minor post-operative tooth sensitivity which usually dissipates in several days to a few weeks
► loss of marginal integrity may lead to recurrent disease |

Endodontics (the Dreaded "Root Canal")

Understandably, root canal therapy does not top anyone's wish list. The procedure, however, has kept the extraction forceps at bay for many damaged teeth and allowed them to function well for years.

In *Chapter 7* the structure of teeth was described in some detail. The soft pulp lives in the core of the tooth, normally protected by mineralized tissues. Pulp is composed mainly of nerves and blood vessels which nourish the few remaining cells in the other tissue layers.

If the integrity of the mineralized layers of the tooth is badly damaged, the pulp is no longer adequately protected. When this occurs, it usually sends out strong and persistent messages of its unhappiness. Anyone who has ever experienced a toothache can testify that it cannot be ignored for long.

Until the 20th century, pulp damage sounded the death knell for the tooth. Enter the endodontist. Practitioners of the discipline of endodontics deal with the tissues inside the tooth, i.e. the pulp.

Research revealed that, devoid of damaged pulp, the tooth could remain disease-free and continue to function normally. Instruments and techniques were designed to remove the damaged or necrotic (dead) pulp tissue from the crown chamber and root canals of the affected tooth. Once emptied, the canals need to be filled with materials to prevent tissue fluids from seeping back into the centre of the tooth.

Endodontically treated teeth function better than artificial replacements. One minor consequence of root canal therapy is the enamel and dentin tissues are somewhat more susceptible to fracture.

For a tooth which requires root canal therapy, this is just the first step in maintaining it. A full-coverage crown for that tooth is in its future. This additional step is needed to protect the tooth from fracture which could make the investment in the root canal therapy worthless.

Tooth Capping (Crowns)

Dental personnel refer to "caps" as "crowns" because the restoration replaces much or all of the tooth crown. One reason for the use of a crown has just been described. Crowns may also be used to restore badly diseased or fractured teeth when the pulp has not been damaged.

Crowns can be made from a variety of materials. The choice depends on the biting forces to which the tooth is subjected and its visibility in the mouth. Molar teeth in the back of the mouth are often restored with metal alloy crowns. These materials withstand heavy biting forces well and are somewhat less expensive to fabricate, since no colour-matching is required.

Highly visible teeth are restored with materials which can be shaded to match the adjacent teeth in the arch. These materials are either specially formulated plastics called acrylics, or porcelain. Where strength and aesthetics are required, crowns can be fabricated with metal alloy cores and porcelain veneers.

Regardless of the type of material chosen, the steps required to complete the crown are the same. When a tooth is prepared for a crown, a portion of the mineralized tissue (enamel and dentin) is removed. The dentist then takes an impression or imprint of the prepared tooth and ships it off to a dental lab where a model is made from it. The lab technician uses the model and with skill and artistry fabricates the crown.

On receiving the finished restoration, the dentist will try the crown on the tooth preparation. If it fits precisely, it will be "cemented" in place. The material used does not act like glue but rather fills in the tiny gap between the inner surface of the crown and the outer surface of the tooth preparation. This prevents saliva and bacteria from leaking under the crown to cause further decay.

If at any time the crown feels loose, or a bad taste from it is noticed, it should be checked immediately. It may mean that the cement seal has been broken and leakage is occurring under the crown. The dentist will check the marginal seal and remove the crown if the seal has been broken. Once off, the tooth will be checked for damage or decay. If the tooth is healthy the remaining cement will be cleaned from the inside of the crown and the fit observed. If all is well, the original crown can be re-cemented. If the tooth has become decayed or fractured it is likely necessary to construct a new crown.

With age, soft tissue tends to "shrink". If this occurs around a crown, the restoration margins might become visible. If this occurs with a back tooth there is no problem. If the crown margins become visible on a front tooth replacement might be considered for aesthetic reasons even if the crown is still functional. A well-fabricated crown in a clean mouth should provide many years of service.

Dental Bridges

If a tooth is lost, especially from a place that doesn't really show, many people may wonder "why bother to replace it?" Perhaps a bridge has been recommended to fill the gap. When advised of the restoration's cost they may have felt it wasn't worth the investment.

Missing teeth should be replaced for sound dental health reasons. Once teeth erupt fully into the mouth, they tend to drift slightly towards the midline of the arches. This drift compensates for wear on the sides of teeth where they touch their neighbours in the arch. Since teeth rub against one another at their contact points during chewing, the side surfaces tend to wear slightly. If teeth did not drift, over time, small spaces would open up between them. When this happens fibrous food tends to pack into these spaces. This food impaction is not only uncomfortable but also injurious to the periodontal tissues around the tooth.

If one or more teeth are removed from any point in the arch, the integrity of the system is broken. Teeth distal (farther from the midline) of the space tend to drift and tilt into the space available. The tooth (or teeth) above the space will move downward as well. Since fewer teeth share the load of mastication (chewing), increased biting forces can over-burden the remaining teeth. Heavy biting forces on poorly positioned teeth increase the potential for destruction of periodontal tissues. Figure 14.1 illustrates this situation.

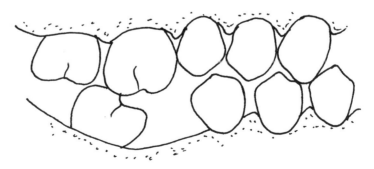

Fig. 14.1. Results of a missing mandibular molar.

Dental bridges are often used to replace single or adjacent missing teeth in one part of the dental arch. Bridgework is appropriate when the following conditions are met:

▶ Teeth are present at both ends of the space.

▶ The teeth on both ends of the space are sound enough to support the required bridge.

▶ The periodontal health of the entire mouth is good (especially around those teeth bordering the space).

▶ The client is willing to take extra measures with plaque control to maintain the bridge once it is placed.

When teeth are missing at the sides or the back of the mouth, a conventional bridge is usually constructed. The teeth on each end of the gap (known as the abutment teeth) are prepared for crowns. An impression is taken of that segment of the arch and sent to the dental lab. As with a crown, a model is made. The technician will prepare patterns of the crowns for the abutment teeth and design a suitable biting surface to bridge the gap between them. The pattern for the entire unit is then used to make the bridge. Figure 14.2 illustrates some posterior bridges.

As with a crown, the dentist will assess the fit of the completed bridge. If adequate, it will be cemented in place. Since the restoration is fixed permanently in place, it closely resembles natural tooth function.

Fig. 14.2. Typical posterior fixed bridges.

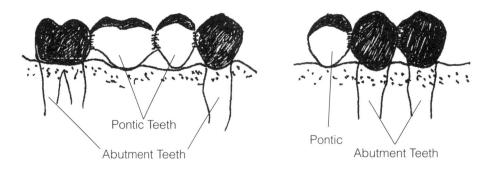

Pontic Teeth

Abutment Teeth

Pontic

Abutment Teeth

Maryland Bridges

The discovery of materials that bond to tooth enamel has lead to the development of a type of bridgework called the Maryland bridge. Although not as popular as it once was, the less invasive preparation for placement makes a Maryland bridge an option as a temporary restoration, especially for young people. When such a bridge is placed for a youngster, it should be replaced with either a conventional bridge or an implant once the complete permanent dentition is stable and the periodontal tissues have reached the contours of adulthood.

These bridges are most useful for replacing a single tooth at the front of the mouth, usually an incisor. They are made of tooth-coloured materials which can be bonded to the healthy enamel tissue. A well-constructed Maryland bridge provides a conservative, aesthetic solution to the problem of a missing front tooth. A small amount of mineralized tissue is removed from the tongue side of the crowns of the teeth at either end of the space. These prepared areas will provide a resting place for extensions on the sides of the false tooth which will fill the gap.

They are not as resistant to damage from biting forces as conventional bridges. A bridge may loosen under normal function, usually because of failure of the bonding material rather than a fracture of the bridge. When this happens, it can be assessed by the dentist and often rebonded in place.

A Maryland bridge could be used to advantage as a temporary restoration in the following situations:

► a single tooth is missing (as in congenital absence of upper lateral incisor teeth)

► the replacement tooth is highly visible

► the tooth is not subjected to heavy biting force

► the teeth on either side of the space are healthy

► the periodontal tissues in the mouth are healthy

► the periodontal tissues cover more of the crown surface (as in a younger person) but will recede somewhat with age.

Dentures as a Solution to Dental Problems

Often, people who have experienced a lot of dental disease in the past, think dentures are the answer. After all, others are wearing them without complaint and they look great. With dentures, no more drilling and filling, no more scraping and polishing.

As with most solutions to problems that seem too good to be true, this one has many negative aspects. Certainly, modern dentistry is able to fabricate the most serviceable dentures ever possible but they are not without drawbacks.

Just as restorative materials are never as functional as healthy tooth structure, dentures cannot reproduce the biting efficiency of a natural, healthy dentition. True, they will not decay, but they will need frequent checking, possible professional cleaning and, over the course of several years, refitting and replacing to maintain maximum efficiency.

There are four basic types of removable dentures available:

- ▶ partial dentures (usually referred to as "partials")

- ▶ complete dentures (sometimes referred to as "plates")

- ▶ overdentures

- ▶ implant-supported dentures

Removable Partial Dentures

Partial dentures are designed to replace several missing teeth in the same arch. They are the treatment of choice where there are insufficient healthy natural teeth remaining to support fixed bridgework.

A partial denture receives some of its support from the underlying mouth tissues and will also attach to the remaining teeth on the end(s) of the space(s). Attachment to abutment teeth helps to stabilize the denture during function and helps to keep it in the mouth.

In some cases, the natural teeth may have suffered loss of supporting periodontal tissues. If so, the denture can be designed to act as a splint to provide support for these teeth.

Figure 14.3 illustrates the components of a typical partial denture described as follows:

▶ A metal framework attaches to the abutment teeth and provides connection between the tooth-bearing segments on the two sides of the dental arch. There is a variety of clasp designs which connect the denture to the remaining teeth.

▶ Acrylic *saddles* support the artificial teeth to fill in the spaces. These plastic areas are molded to conform to the contours of the underlying tissues. When the denture is in function, the biting forces are carried by the remaining bone under the denture saddles and by the abutment teeth.

▶ Denture teeth made of acrylic: front denture teeth resemble natural ones in all aspects. Back denture teeth resemble natural ones in most aspects. The biting surfaces may vary. Some denture teeth are sculpted with elevations and grooves to duplicate natural teeth. Others have smooth biting surfaces. Those with smooth chewing surfaces are used where retention of the denture may be poor. Smoother surfaces contacting each other help keep the denture in place while chewing.

Fig. 14.3. Example of an upper partial denture.

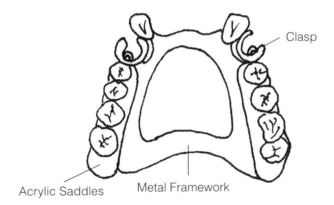

When multiple teeth are missing, the dentist is the best source of information regarding choices of suitable restorations. Table 14.2 gives some general guidelines regarding who might consider partial dentures and those who would not be ideal candidates for this option.

Table 14.2
Factors Favouring the Choice of Partial Dentures
► several teeth are missing on the same side, or on both sides of the dental arch
► as a temporary replacement for multiple missing primary teeth in a child (the appliance will have to be modified as the child grows)
► as a temporary replacement for a small number of teeth in an adolescent (the removal of extensive tooth structure to fabricate fixed bridgework can be postponed until the individual is older)
► for people who cannot tolerate the longer appointments necessary to prepare the mouth for bridges or implants
► to incorporate a splint into the restoration to support remaining teeth
Factors Against the Choice of Partial Dentures
► lack of a suitable number of teeth to support the denture
► severe decay in the remaining teeth which may compromise their retention even after restoration
► severe bone loss around the remaining teeth which leaves them unable to support a partial, even with splinting options incorporated into the denture
► the client does not like the appearance of the partial and its required clasps which may be visible on the remaining teeth
► the client finds it difficult to perform adequate daily oral hygiene of the remaining teeth

Fitting of partial dentures requires, on average, a series of at least five appointments after the initial examination and consultation. If the remaining teeth need attention, cleaning and/or restorations, additional appointments will be needed.

Appointment Sequence for Fitting of Partial Dentures

1. Preliminary impressions or imprints are taken of the mouth in order to make models for the dentist to study. This three-dimensional representation of the mouth allows him/her to design the dentures needed. Sometimes special impression trays are constructed on this model for use at the second appointment.

2. During the second appointment the final impressions are taken. These are used to pour the cast on which the denture will be made. The technician will use this cast to make a wax model of the denture framework which includes blocks in the areas of the missing teeth or have denture teeth set in wax.

3. At the third appointment, the dentist will have the client try the wax model of the denture in his/her mouth. The location of the artificial teeth will then be marked out for the technician to follow when the model is returned to the lab. Once at the lab, the wax model material will be replaced with the metal, acrylic and appropriate artificial teeth of the designed denture.

4. At the fourth appointment the client receives the new denture. Sometimes minor adjustments have to be made to ensure that it fits properly. Instruction in its insertion, removal and general care will be provided.

5. Often further appointments are required to make additional adjustments. Until clients get used to handling their dentures, they may unwittingly cause distortion of the clasps when inserting or removing them. If insertion or removal is difficult, trying to force it to fit may cause more serious damage to the framework or clasps. The dentist should be consulted to adjust the denture for easier handling.

Complete Dentures

For those who have already lost all of their teeth in one or both arches, complete dentures are necessary. People sometimes refer to them as "plates".

Modern materials available can make very aesthetically pleasing dentures. However, the chewing efficiency of even the best-constructed false teeth falls vastly short of the natural dentition. For this reason, dentists are very hesitant to recommend complete dentures as a restorative measure unless it is the last resort.

The normal periodontal, or supporting, structures of teeth are described in *Chapter 8*. The alveolar bone, which forms the tooth sockets and supports the teeth, exists only as long as teeth are present. Once a tooth is lost, that portion of the alveolar ridge is absorbed by body cells. If all of the teeth in an arch are removed, over time, the alveolar ridge shrinks. This results in dentures becoming loose and less efficient. If the ridge becomes very shallow, it may not be possible to design a denture with adequate retention for function.

It is easier to compensate for loss of supporting bone under an upper denture. In addition to underlying bone support, upper dentures are stabilized by suction present between the denture base and the palate. No such suction is available in the lower arch. In addition, normal movements of the tongue make lower denture retention more difficult. Early loss of mandibular teeth may result in inability to retain a traditionally designed lower denture later in life.

Facial muscle balance is also important to the retention and function of complete dentures. Conversely, facial muscle tics or eccentric habits may have a negative impact on the ability to wear complete dentures successfully. Slack facial muscles may also lead to poor denture retention.

Figure 14.4 illustrates the components of a typical complete denture described as follows:

▶ The denture base is in contact with the underlying mouth tissues. Denture base material is acrylic which can be molded and tinted realistically to reproduce the gum tissue around the teeth. Sometimes, areas of the denture base are reinforced with metal alloy under the acrylic for strength and retention of the artificial teeth.

▶ The denture teeth themselves: complete-denture teeth are the same as those used to make partial dentures as already described.

Fig. 14.4. Complete upper and lower dentures.

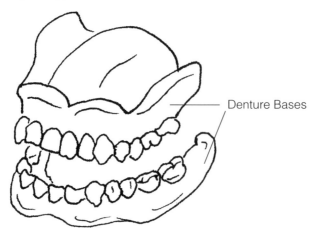

Denture Bases

There are two ways of delivering a complete denture. For clients who have been without all their teeth for some time, the tissues will have healed and their dentures can often be constructed and delivered without further dental treatment. If clients are making the decision to acquire a complete denture they may still have teeth remaining. Usually the teeth present are those in the front of the mouth and occasionally a few at the back.

If this is the case, the dentist will probably offer the option of an "immediate" denture (especially if the one contemplated is for the upper arch). The dentist takes the required impressions and gets the lab work completed. (The appointment sequence for full denture construction is described later in this chapter.)

Once the denture is received from the lab, an appointment will be arranged for removal of the remaining teeth and the denture will be inserted at that time. Instructions on when and how to remove it and care for the appliance and the underlying tissue as healing takes place will be provided.

It is important to remember, that as healing occurs, the underlying tissue contour will change. Further appointments will be needed to reline the denture to ensure that it conforms properly to the tissue once healing is complete. Unless this is done, the denture will never work to best advantage. These appointments will occur over several weeks to months after initial insertion of the denture.

Appointment Sequence for Fitting of Complete Dentures

1. Preliminary impressions or imprints are taken of the mouth in order to make models for the dentist to study so that appropriate appliances can be designed. Special impression trays are then constructed on this model for use at the second appointment.

2. During the second appointment the final impressions are taken of the mouth. These are used to make the model on which the denture will be made. The technician returns a wax model of the denture base which includes blocks in the areas where artificial teeth will be placed. The dentist will determine the tooth placement for the lab technician.

3. At the third appointment, the dentist will have the client try the wax model of the denture with the artificial teeth set in place. Any adjustments are made and the denture model is returned to the lab. The technician will replace the wax holding the artificial teeth with acrylic base material, then finish and polish the denture.

4. The fourth appointment is the one at which any remaining teeth will be removed and the denture inserted. The dentist will probably schedule at least one post-operative appointment to check on the progress of healing. Sometimes, minor adjustments to the denture are required at this time.

5. Further appointments are required a few weeks or months later to check the fit of the denture. As the tissue heals the denture may need to be relined so that it fits the changed contours of the underlying tissue.

Overdentures

Although this procedure can be considered in either dental arch, it is more frequently carried out for mandibular (lower arch) dentures. Since the stability of a lower complete denture depends on the presence of an adequate bony ridge and alveolar bone depends on the presence of teeth, most dentists will try to avoid making a complete lower denture whenever possible. If even one or two teeth are left in the arch with healthy root structure and supporting bone, construction of an overdenture can be considered.

Where an overdenture is the appropriate choice, the dentist will remove the crown bulk from the remaining teeth and cover the preparations with a cast metal coping. Root canal therapy may also be needed for these teeth. The steps in denture construction are then the same as previously described. The resulting appliance will resemble a typical complete denture and will fit over the coping on the remaining teeth. Ability to use remaining teeth in this manner to support a complete denture (especially if it is for the lower arch) improves its stability and efficiency significantly.

Implant-supported Restorations

The development of materials (usually titanium) that can be embedded in alveolar bone has expanded restorative treatment options for missing teeth. These devices are referred to as dental implants. An implant consists of three parts:

▶ the implant or anchor portion which is embedded in the alveolar bone

▶ the abutment screw used to connect the replacement tooth or appliance to the implant

▶ the abutment post or cylinder that attaches the restoration to the screw.

Two surgical procedures are required to place implants. During the first, the soft tissue will be incised and the bone prepared to receive the metal device. Once placed in the bone, the soft tissue will be closed over the implant and stitched in place. The metal implant will bond with the bone in three to six months.

During the second surgery, the soft tissue is removed from the implant anchor and the abutment portion which will protrude above the gum tissue and support the restoration is attached to it. Again, soft tissue healing must occur before insertion of the finished restoration or appliance.

Some general practice dentists have taken the additional training necessary to carry out the surgical implant procedures. Others may refer the client to a specialist, either a periodontist or an oral surgeon who has the required expertise.

The complexity of this treatment, the increased vigilance with home care required and the substantial financial investment means it is not suitable for everyone. Ideal candidates are those who are in good general health, have sufficient underlying bone and are willing to maintain scrupulous oral hygiene and attend regular dental visits for assistance in maintaining the appliance. If after a comprehensive evaluation, client and dentist feel it is an appropriate treatment choice, the appointment sequence can occur.

Single Tooth Replacement

For appropriate candidates, implants can be used successfully to replace a single tooth anywhere in the arch. Using an implant-supported false tooth means that teeth adjacent to the space do not have to be manipulated to support the restoration. Figure 14.5A shows replacement of a single tooth with an implant-supported crown.

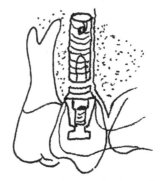

Fig. 14.5A. Implant-supported crown to replace a single tooth.

Multiple Teeth Replacement

Implants can also be used to support fixed bridgework. In addition to the advantage of non-interference with adjacent healthy teeth, implant-supported bridges can also be used where teeth are not available on both ends of the space created by the missing teeth. These situations are illustrated in figures 14.5B and 14.5C.

Fig. 14.5B. Implant-supported posterior fixed bridge.

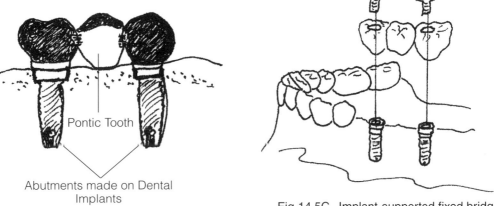

Pontic Tooth

Abutments made on Dental Implants

Fig.14.5C. Implant-supported fixed bridge.

Dentures

For clients who are likely to have difficulty wearing a conventional full lower denture and yet do not have any remaining teeth to support an overdenture, the dentist may recommend placement of implants before a denture is made. Perhaps someone has been wearing a full lower denture for some years and adjustments no longer improve its stability in the mouth. In such a case the dentist may now propose an implant-supported denture. Figure 14.5D illustrates the components of an implant-supported denture as described in the following paragraphs.

Metal posts will be embedded into the remaining bone in strategic places in the dental arches. These metal devices bond with the bone and provide support for a complete denture in the same manner as retained teeth support an overdenture.

Acquiring an implant-supported denture is not as straightforward as the fitting of a conventional denture. There are three distinct phases to undergo:

▶   the surgical implanting of the anchorage devices and subsequent healing

▶   attachment of the abutment portions of the device and subsequent healing

▶   construction of the denture once healing of tissues has occurred.

The time lapse, from initial consultation to new denture insertion, may be as long as three to nine months. During that time clients may be able to wear the old denture which the dentist has modified.

Fig. 14.5D. Implant-supported complete lower denture.

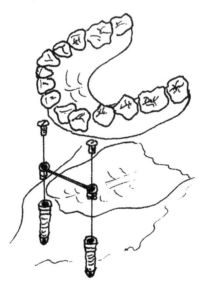

Chapter 15

Behind the Hollywood Smile – Cosmetic Procedures

In This Chapter

- ▶ history of tooth whitening
- ▶ common causes of tooth discolouration
- ▶ whitening of healthy teeth (vital bleaching)
- ▶ professionally applied in-office procedures
- ▶ dentist-prescribed home-applied treatments
- ▶ potential side effects of tooth-whitening procedures
- ▶ pre-bleaching checklist
- ▶ whitening of non-vital teeth
- ▶ cosmetic veneers

History of Tooth Whitening

Throughout history, people have considered white teeth beautiful. In the 21st century the trend continues. In the past several years many products have been developed which are advertised to take years off your smile.

Tooth whitening (or vital-tooth bleaching) refers to procedures designed to lighten the colour of normal healthy tooth enamel without surgical or restorative intervention. The aim is to achieve the desired colour without harming the tooth or other mouth tissues. Many of these products have been marketed recently enough that long-term safety of their effects has yet to be determined.

The evolution of tooth-whitening procedures began in 1937 (coincident with the burgeoning Hollywood film industry producing motion pictures in colour with their own sound tracks). At that time strong chemical oxidizing agents and heat were applied to teeth to obtain favourable colour changes. Some of the chemicals used then and now have been identified as carcinogens.

Considerable improvements to the system were discovered somewhat accidentally in the 1970s by two Arkansas dentists, Dr. Bill Klusmier and Dr. Jerry Wagner. Both had been using 10 percent carbamide peroxide solution to treat their clients' canker sores and observed that a side effect of treatment was a lightening in tooth colour.

In 1988 Dr. Van B. Haywood and Dr. Harald Heymann conducted formal laboratory and clinical studies in vital-tooth bleaching. Ongoing research indicates that, generally speaking, tooth-whitening procedures are safe. Studies also indicate the procedures to be from 75-97 percent effective, depending on the type of discolouration present and the way the agent is applied. Results of the process may last from one to seven years.

Common Causes of Tooth Discolouration

There are two basic types of tooth discolouration. The first type, referred to as extrinsic, includes all stains that are restricted to the cracks and crannies in the surface of tooth enamel. This category includes discolouration caused by smoking and ingestion of foods and beverages that stain tooth surfaces. Chromogenic (colour-producing) bacteria living in the mouth also contribute to a buildup of extrinsic stain, as do some nutritional supplements that contain iron compounds. Daily oral hygiene practices and routine professional cleaning keep extrinsic stain under control to a significant degree.

The second category, known as *intrinsic*, includes tooth discolouration that is an integral part of the structure of tooth enamel. Common causes are:

► excessive amounts of systemic fluoride available during the time of enamel formation of tooth development

► administration of tetracycline antibiotics during tooth development (no longer prescribed for this age group, other antibiotics are now used which do not have this side effect)

► normal aging processes. As teeth age, the enamel covering becomes more translucent. This allows the darker-coloured dentin which underlies the enamel to become more visible. Consequently teeth appear greyer or more yellow with age. Colour changes associated with aging are difficult to reverse.

► endodontic therapy occasionally leaves teeth discoloured. These non-vital teeth can also be whitened. Procedures to do so are described later in this chapter.

Whitening of Healthy Teeth (Vital Bleaching)

Although the mechanisms of bleaching a vital tooth (i.e. the nerve is "alive") are not completely understood it appears to be related to oxidation and the interaction of compounds of oxygen with the enamel surface. For this reason, agents which create colour change are those that oxidize readily. Active ingredients in tooth-whitening products are usually hydrogen peroxide or carbamide peroxide (where a 3 percent solution of hydrogen peroxide is similar in effectiveness to a 10 percent solution of carbamide peroxide).

Depending on the product and mode of delivery, other ingredients may be included such as glycerin, carbopol (a slower oxygen-releasing formula), sodium hydroxide, fluoride and flavouring.

Vital bleaching may be carried out by professional application of agents in-office or by self-administration using the over-the-counter (OTC) products available.

Professionally Applied In-office Procedures

Professionally delivered tooth-whitening procedures are sometimes referred to as "power bleaching". Dental practitioners are allowed to use much higher concentration of solutions of bleaching products than are available over the counter. Professionally applied products may contain 35 percent or more of the active whitening agent.

The higher concentration of solutions dictates precise application of the product. The practitioner will ensure the teeth are isolated and soft tissues of the mouth protected before the agent is placed on the surfaces to be whitened. The higher solution concentration results in more rapid colour changes. One office visit may be sufficient to obtain the desired effect. If stains are resistant, more visits may be required.

The downside of professional bleaching is cost – considerably more than self-applied OTC methods. Since tooth whitening is considered a cosmetic procedure insurance companies will not provide coverage for it

In-office bleaching procedures may also include the use of lasers to speed up the reaction of the oxidizing agent. Isolation procedures necessary for tissue protection during laser assisted treatment need to be precise making the process somewhat time-consuming. Although this technique is the most costly of all bleaching procedures, it produces the most rapid results.

Dentist-prescribed Home-applied Treatments

Tray Methods

A more cost effective approach to tooth whitening is a combination of professional supervision and self-treatment. With this option, the dental practitioner will take impressions of the teeth and create models of the arches. These models are then used to fabricate small, flexible custom-fitted trays. Since these trays control the flow of material effectively, the agent prescribed for use is usually a slightly higher concentration (5-10 percent solutions) than that provided in OTC products.

The client places the product in the trays and wears them as directed (usually overnight) for a period of one to six weeks. Some resistant areas may require longer treatment. Results can be expected to last from one to three years.

Strip Application

Professionally prescribed whitening products embedded in flexible plastic strips for home application contain 6.5-14 percent hydrogen peroxide as the active ingredient. Standard OTC products supply agents at up to 6 percent concentration. These strips are usually used nightly for one to three weeks. The main disadvantages of this mode of delivery are poorer tooth coverage and increased potential for dislodging the strip during wear. These may be offset in the user's eyes by the convenience, ease of use, and reduced cost.

Usually the models in tooth-care product commercials have textbook smiles. If teeth are crowded, tipped or rotated, application and retention of tooth-whitening strips may be something of a problem. When teeth are rotated or crowded, brush-on products might make application easier and provide better coverage to create a more pleasing result.

Brush-on Technique

Although various formulations of brush-on whitening agents are now available, they are less popular than the strip- or tray-applied materials. The active ingredient is combined with polymers in gel form that adheres to teeth. These OTC products are self-applied. The adhesive quality of the product allows the active ingredient sustained opportunity to penetrate the tooth enamel to remove surface and embedded stains.

Brush-on formulations include products with the following active ingredients: 6.7 percent hydrogen peroxide, 19 percent sodium percarbonate peroxide and 18 percent carbamide peroxide.

Potential Side Effects of Tooth-whitening Procedures

Tooth Sensitivity

Some people report short-term tooth sensitivity to temperature changes. This is more likely to occur in teeth where gingival (gum tissue) recession has exposed part of the root surface. Sensitivity may occur during the period of tray wear or upon tray removal.

Remedies for sensitivity include:

▶ terminating the whitening treatment

▶ reducing the wearing period of the trays or strips

▶ alternating the use of the bleaching product with a desensitizing solution (potassium nitrate or fluoride). Some bleaching systems include a desensitizing product in the kit. Fluoride mouthrinses are also available over the counter and, when used as directed, may reduce sensitivity during and after the bleaching process

Gingival Irritation

Irritation of soft tissue usually occurs when the bleaching product comes in prolonged contact with the gingiva (gum tissue). The usual cause is a poorly fitted tray. Since OTC tray-applied materials do not provide a custom-fitted appliance, the potential for gingival irritation is higher with these products.

OTC strip-applied products have somewhat less potential for causing gingival irritation because they contain active ingredients that are less fluid and the strips are designed to cover fewer teeth.

Pre-bleaching Checklist

If you are contemplating whiter teeth, consider the following:

▶ Am I in good general health?

▶ Do I have teeth with exposed roots?

▶ Are any of my teeth currently sensitive to temperature changes?

Before embarking on any type of tooth-whitening program you should have your teeth examined and cleaned. Your dentist will also check for tooth decay, faulty restorations and periodontal disease. If a professional cleaning has not been part of your oral care routine, you may be happy with the results.

Your dental practitioner can advise you on whether or not additional tooth-whitening procedures are suitable for you. If you already have composite resin restorations in your mouth that match your current tooth colour, remember that bleaching procedures will affect only tooth enamel, not the fillings. If you alter the shade of your teeth significantly, your tooth-coloured restorations may need to be replaced.

If you have worn composite restorations slated for replacement and you are a candidate for bleaching procedures, postpone the restorative treatment until your teeth have reached their new shade.

Whitening of Non-vital Teeth

Often healthy teeth, particularly front ones, can sustain blows that do not cause obvious outward damage. However, the pulp may be traumatized to the point of no recovery. Since the tooth is otherwise healthy, the treatment of choice is endodontic therapy to remove the damaged pulp tissue.

The pulp canal can usually be cleaned out through a small hole in the tongue side (lingual surface) of the tooth crown. The only restoration required is a little filling that doesn't even show. In such cases a side effect of the trauma and resulting treatment can be permanent internal staining.

Tooth colour can often be improved in these cases using in-office bleaching procedures for non-vital teeth. During this procedure the dentist will remove the restoration and the filling material in the crown portion of the pulp canal. The power-bleaching agent (often 35 percent hydrogen peroxide) is then placed inside the tooth. When sufficient whitening has occurred, the pulp chamber is rinsed thoroughly and a white composite core is placed into the chamber. The lingual surface is then sealed with a suitably tinted composite resin restoration.

Cosmetic Veneers

Prior to the development of bleaching agents, the only sure way to create a significant change in tooth colour was restorative intervention. At first this meant preparing the whole tooth crown to receive a "cap" or crown. For details on this procedure please refer to *Chapter 14*. With the development of materials that adhere to tooth structure, cosmetic colour change to specific teeth can be accomplished with application of veneers. The word as used in dentistry means the same as it does in other applications, i.e. the attachment of a thin layer of material (in this case tooth-coloured composite resin or porcelain) to a prepared base.

Veneers may be used when vital bleaching may not create the desired results. Reasons for selecting veneers as a treatment choice include:

▶ improving the colour of teeth that are seriously stained or deformed by fluorosis or tetracycline stain

▶ increasing the size of the crowns of teeth to close spaces between front teeth which the client may consider unsightly

▶ improving the appearance of minor tooth malposition by recontouring tooth crowns to change the alignment of anterior teeth.

There are two techniques used to apply cosmetic veneers. The direct technique places the veneer material directly on the client's teeth; indirect technique uses veneers produced in the dental laboratory and bonded in place.

Direct Veneer Placement

Using this technique, the dentist can accomplish the procedure in one appointment. The first step is to select an appropriate shade of material. The teeth are then isolated (using a rubber dam or cotton rolls to provide access and a dry field) and prepared. A very thin layer of enamel is removed from the surface to receive the veneer. Usually local anaesthetic is not required.

A preformed plastic crown form is selected and tried on the tooth for size. It is trimmed as necessary to create an appropriate fit. The tooth surface is then etched with a mild solution of acid, rinsed, dried and an acrylic sealant material is painted into the etched surface. If the tooth enamel is darkly stained, an opaque agent may be placed first to prevent the appearance of a dark shadow under the more translucent veneer product. The sealant material adheres to the tooth surface and acts as a chemically bonded interface with the composite resin that makes up the veneer.

The veneer material is placed in the crown form and fitted back on the sealed tooth. When the resin is hard, the crown form will be removed. All that is left for the dentist to do is trim away any excess resin, contour the surface and polish the new veneer.

Indirect Technique

Since this technique requires fabrication of the veneers in a dental lab, at least two appointments are necessary. At the first, the shade will be selected and the tooth surfaces prepared as described above. An impression will be taken of the prepared teeth and forwarded to the dental lab. A model will be made and the lab technician will create the veneers (usually from porcelain) and return them to the dentist.

At the second appointment, the dentist will check the fit and colour of the veneers. If all is well, the teeth will be isolated, etched, rinsed and sealed as described earlier. If opaquing material is required, this is placed as well. Bonding material is then applied to the inside of the veneer to bond the restoration chemically to the sealant material.

After the bonding agent sets, removal of excess material and final trimming of the veneer is completed.

Veneers – Care and Cautions

Like all restorations, there is a margin at which the veneer meets the tooth surface. Excellent daily oral self care is necessary to keep veneer surfaces and margins free of bacterial plaque and stain buildup. Since veneers do not have the same resistance to biting forces as normal tooth tissue, biting into hard candies, nuts or vegetables may cause the bond between the tooth and material to fail or fracture the veneer itself.

Even with the best of care, veneers have a limited life span: a range of about seven to 15 years. Longevity depends on the level of home care the client practices as well as diet. Clients who smoke, drink excessive amounts of tea, coffee and red wine or who are not careful with daily oral hygiene will find their veneers will stain.

When veneers become chipped, worn or seriously discoloured they will need replacement. With increasing age, some degree of gingival (gum tissue) recession occurs in most people. This may make the margins of the veneer quite visible. When this occurs, if cosmetic improvement is desired, the veneer will have to be replaced.

Part VII

Dental Emergencies and Other Stuff

Chapter 16

Emergencies, X-rays, Access to Information, Oral Piercing

In This Chapter

▶ coping with dental emergencies
▶ dental x-rays
▶ who owns dental records?
▶ oral piercing

Coping with Dental Emergencies

Lost or Broken Orthodontic Appliances

If you lose or break any part of your orthodontic appliance more than a couple of days before your regular appointment, call the office for an extra visit. If you can remove the offending bits or cover the sharp edges with wax you can probably hold out for a day or two. It is wise to advise the office in advance that you are coming in with appliances needing repair. Then the staff knows your appointment will need to be a little longer.

Broken arch wires, a head gear which doesn't fit, lost elastics which tie the arch wire to the brackets, loose bands, or brackets that have come off mean the appliance is not functioning properly and should be repaired. At least, the teeth affected by the broken segment of the appliance will not be moving; at most, the broken elements of the system could cause discomfort and damage to teeth or soft tissue.

Lost Restorations

With wear and tear, all dental restorations lose integrity at their margins with the tooth tissue. In other words, the filling does not contact the tooth completely. Some restorative materials are more susceptible to this damage than others. When marginal integrity is lost, bacterial plaque is more likely to form in the crevice created. Where there are bacteria and food debris present, there will be the potential for recurrent tooth decay around the restoration. If recurrent decay becomes established, the restoration can loosen and eventually be lost. Usually these events occur when you are about to leave home or are on vacation in a foreign land.

Loss of the filling can leave the tooth sensitive to temperature changes and the sharp edges of the cavity will draw your tongue like a magnet. In the short term there is probably little danger to survival of the tooth. If you are at home, call your dentist, chew on the other side of your mouth and keep the area clean for a day or so until an appointment can be scheduled.

If you happen to be far from home for a few more weeks, when you find a dentist willing to see you, you are probably safe in requesting placement of a temporary restoration. These filling materials, known as dental cements, will keep out food debris and bacteria and provide a reasonably hearty filling for periods of up to several weeks. You can have the permanent restoration placed by your own dentist when you get home. If, during the interval, the tooth becomes sensitive, especially to heat, it should be examined again as immediate attention may be required.

Tooth Fractures

A tooth that already has a large restoration in it can fracture when you crunch something hard unexpectedly. If it is not uncomfortable, call your dentist and have it checked as soon as it is mutually convenient.

Other tooth fractures occur as a result of trauma – often as sports related injuries. The easiest way to deal with them is through prevention by using face and mouth protection suitable to the sport. While such protection is usually mandatory during league play (hockey, baseball, etc.) road hockey and informal sandlot games claim their share of victims as players leave protective gear behind.

If the fracture involves only a small chip with a rough edge, the solution is a quick trip to the dentist and a little grinding of the enamel to smooth the edge. Fractures that expose dentin tissue leave the tooth sensitive and should be investigated quickly. If the fracture exposes the pulp, this is an emergency requiring dental attention as soon as possible.

Traumatic Injuries – Tooth Intrusion or Evulsion

Accidents resulting in tooth loss and soft tissue damage to the face are also true dental emergencies. All tend to be frightening to the person sustaining them, and to those watching, due to immediate flow of blood. Tissues of the mouth and face are highly vascular and can bleed profusely with little apparent damage.

Use clean material (gauze or facial tissue, etc.) to place direct pressure on the wound to stem the blood flow and assist in the initiation of a clot. Seek medical or dental assistance as quickly as possible.

Often a blow to the face will cause *intrusion* or *evulsion* of a tooth or teeth. Intrusion can occur when your toddler trips and falls face first into the corner of the coffee table. The blow may cause one or more of the front teeth to be shoved up into the gum tissue. The accident may also cause the teeth to cut the lip. Bleeding and swelling will occur very quickly. Apply pressure to stop the bleeding and seek professional help immediately. It is important to locate the teeth (either in or out of the child's mouth) and check the soft tissue. Until the teeth can be accounted for, it is assumed they were perhaps swallowed or aspirated (breathed into the lung). Of the two possibilities, aspiration is much more serious. Some sutures (stitches) may be necessary to assist the healing of the soft tissue. The dentist will probably take x-rays to locate the teeth if they are still in the mouth, and to see whether or not deeper damage has been done to underlying bone and the developing permanent teeth.

If older children or adults fall or are hit in the face, teeth are more likely to be evulsed, (knocked out). Evulsed teeth often remain intact and, if professional help is readily available, can be implanted and returned to function. When a tooth is evulsed it is important to find it to verify that it has not been swallowed or aspirated. Once found, check it to see if it is whole and without obvious fractures.

The tooth may not survive implantation, but the sooner it is returned to the mouth the greater the chance of success. If the tooth is relatively clean, replace it in the socket and then head to the dental office. If you (or a companion) are too squeamish to do this, and that is certainly understandable, put the tooth in its owner's mouth to keep it moist, or the next best option is to soak it in a small jar of milk if some is readily available. For successful implantation, time is critical. Each minute the tooth is out of its environment reduces the chances of successful reattachment.

Any dental office that knows you are on the way with this problem will give you top priority on arrival. If the tooth is in good shape, the dentist will put it back into its socket and wire it to adjacent teeth for stability. A short course of antibiotics may be prescribed to ward off infection. Now the waiting game begins. If the tooth is going to be rejected, it will be obvious within a few days. If the surrounding tissue begins to heal, chances are good reattachment is taking place. When the periodontal tissue is healthy, the tooth will require root canal treatment. With prompt action and a bit of luck, some implanted teeth function normally for years.

If implantation is not a preferred action, there are other treatment options with reliable and excellent outcomes.

Toothaches

Most serious toothaches occur when tooth decay has progressed to the point of exposing the inner pulp tissue to exterior stimulation such as heat, cold, air, pressure, etc.

Since dental decay is generally a slowly progressing disease, it can be long-standing before any pain is felt. If you find yourself in the unfortunate situation of experiencing a toothache, most dentists you contact for assistance will make every attempt to see you as quickly as possible, whether or not you are a client in the practice. If you are in an urban area and not sure how to find help, look in the phone book under "dental emergencies" for contact numbers to direct you to care.

Usually you are better off not self-medicating to try to relieve the pain. Depending on the remedy you have chosen, the dentist may be hampered in beginning appropriate treatment until the drugs you have chosen clear your system.

On completion of assessment of your general and oral health, you will be offered treatment options to relieve the problem.

Dental X-rays

Discovery

Wilhelm Conrad Röentgen's discovery of x-rays in the autumn of 1895 changed the world of medicine and dentistry forever. By 1896, this energy had been harnessed and was already providing practitioners with something they never dreamed possible – the ability to see an image of internal body parts and tissues without surgical invasion. The therapeutic benefits of radiation in cancer treatment were discovered later.

As with all new discoveries, x-rays proved to be a two-edged sword. Their benefits as an imaging tool were immediately obvious and x-rays were used without caution for years. Gradually it became obvious that too much of a good thing is in fact a bad thing. Radiation could help cure but it could also cause irreparable damage.

Discovering the potential harm of overexposure to x-rays created awareness that their controlled use was necessary. The goal of such control is to ensure every time radiation is used for diagnosis or treatment, the potential benefit to the client outweighs potential harm.

Control

Since 1980, Ontario, Canada, is a jurisdiction that has had comprehensive legislation regarding the use of diagnostic and therapeutic radiation. The government considered this legislation important because the world is full of sources of radiation beyond human control. These sources include: cosmic radiation from space; gamma radiation from soil; natural radionuclides incorporated into the body and radon gases in air.

Artificially produced radiation is controllable. The *Healing Arts Radiation Protection Act* (commonly referred to by Ontarians as *HARP*) defines the legal use of x-rays for diagnosis and treatment.

This comprehensive law addresses the following:

▶ who is entitled to own x-ray equipment

▶ standards of installation and maintenance of diagnostic and therapeutic x-ray equipment

▶ designation and qualifications of personnel responsible for installation and maintenance of equipment

▶ designation of practitioners qualified to prescribe x-rays for diagnosis or treatment

▶ circumstances under which radiation can be prescribed

▶ designation of practitioners entitled to operate diagnostic and therapeutic x-ray machines

▶ approval of curriculum used to prepare operators of x-ray equipment

▶ actions to be taken if the law is broken.

In the past dentists tended to view taking of x-rays as a "routine procedure". Their clients had them taken according to a defined time interval. Some practitioners considered all clients with complete permanent dentitions should have x-rays taken once a year; some even considered every six months was appropriate. In Ontario, under *HARP*, x-rays prescribed by the calendar are no longer legal.

According to this legislation diagnostic radiation is **not** to be prescribed prior to clinical examination and determination of need. This is to ensure every x-ray taken is justified: minimum exposure for maximum benefit. For regular clients in the practice, the interval of need may be pre-determined by the dentist based on the client's known dental history and oral self-care practices.

In dentistry, two basic types of x-rays are taken: intra-oral (where the film recording the image is placed in the client's mouth) and extra-oral (where the film is held outside the mouth). For many years the permanent image was recorded on the exposed film by soaking it in developer and fixer chemical solutions followed by rinsing and drying. This procedure creates a delay in the ability to use the x-rays after they are exposed. Today, instant radiographic images can be captured digitally and stored on a computer for future reference or for the creation of a hard copy of the image.

Indications for Use of Diagnostic X-rays in Dentistry

Dentists prescribe x-rays as an important tool for providing excellent disease prevention services and competent dental treatment. Proper exposure techniques make the risk of damage infinitesimal. The profession likes to keep the risk at that level by using radiation wisely.

Prescribed x-rays are an important part of dental care under the following circumstances:

► Children may need a small number of x-rays taken during replacement of their baby teeth with permanent ones just to ensure that growth and development are proceeding normally.

► X-rays are an essential part of diagnosis and treatment of malocclusions (crooked teeth).

► Once all the permanent teeth are in place, x-rays of the back teeth are required occasionally to check for decay of abutting tooth surfaces. If you have frequently experienced decay, x-rays will be required more often until the disease is under control.

► Individuals with a large number of restorations in the sides of their teeth may require x-rays more frequently as the fillings age and wear.

► If you report mouth pain and the cause is not immediately obvious, x-rays will assist in the diagnosis of the problem.

► X-rays are required prior to the extraction of teeth to give the dentist better information about the oral anatomy of the surgical site prior to the procedure.

► If you develop periodontal disease, x-rays will be required to assess bone loss and regeneration in response to treatment.

Who Owns Dental Records?

You may think that because you have paid for the services, your records are yours. All medical and dental records, including x-rays (radiographs), are the property of the practitioner who has collected and used the data for your care. They are part of the clinical records practitioners must maintain concerning the clients they see.

Standards for records maintenance are set out in health legislation of the jurisdiction where the practice is established. The legislation is further interpreted by the governing body of the professional who uses them. Practitioners who disregard these standards commit legal infractions of practice and can be held accountable for records mismanagement. Although standards vary, many jurisdictions require that professional records be maintained on clients for at least 10 years from the date of the last visit or until the death of the client.

All medical and dental records are confidential. Under specific federal and provincial (state) legislation the information they contain can only be shared with other professionals on a "need to know" basis with the written consent of the client to whom they pertain. If you are being referred to a specialist for treatment, your general practitioner will forward any pertinent information and x-rays to him/her. If you choose to become established with a new practitioner, you have the right to request your previous dentist transfer copies of your treatment records to the new office. A reasonable fee can be charged for this service.

In most jurisdictions, you also have the right to know what information is contained in your medical and dental records. Practitioners cannot unreasonably refuse you copies of the information they contain. They have the right to apply a reasonable charge for providing this service to you.

Oral Piercing

If you are determined to go ahead with having your lips or tongue pierced, you should at least consider the physiological risks involved with this action. Some of the potential problems with oral jewelry are described below.

Infection

The mouth is one area of the body which carries a heavy bacterial load. Even with excellent hygiene, many strains of bacteria live in abundance in the oral cavity. Any object, including rings and bars used in oral piercing, provide additional, difficult-to-clean surfaces on which oral bacteria colonize. Foreign intra-oral objects also increase the potential for laceration or abrasion of soft tissue in the mouth.

Breaks in the oral mucosa (skin in the mouth) provide an opportunity for infection to occur at the site. When skin is damaged bacteria can also access the bloodstream and travel throughout the body. If you are in good general health, such infections may be minor. If you are, or become, immuno-suppressed (as a result of HIV infection, treatment for various diseases or because of organ transplant medications), these infections of oral origin could become serious or life threatening.

The risk of infection is most acute at the time the piercing is done and until the wound heals. Owners of piercing operations may be less diligent about cleanliness than they should be. With inadequate sterilization of piercing equipment serious infections such as hepatitis or, less likely, HIV/AIDS could result.

Periodontal Disease and Tooth Fracture

Depending on the type of jewelry placed and its location, normal movements of the lips and tongue may bring the device into contact with soft gingival tissues in an adverse manner. In response to the trauma, gingival tissue may become bruised, lacerated, infected, or simply recede from the abuse. If gingival tissue recedes, the underlying bone supporting the tooth disappears as well. Exposed tooth roots can become sensitive and are more vulnerable to abrasion and decay. Once periodontal tissue (gingiva and bone) are gone, they will not regenerate. Periodontal grafts may be necessary to stabilize the damage. Periodontal surgery is expensive.

Tooth fractures resulting from placement of tongue barbells are reported with increasing frequency in dental literature as negative side effects of oral piercing. Plastic or rubber ends on tongue barbells may somewhat reduce the potential for damage. Tooth fractures caused by oral jewelry often require complex and expensive restorations such as crowns to repair the damage.

Consider one last caution. You may think oral piercing is completely reversible: when you get tired of it, take out the jewelry with no long-term consequences. Unfortunately, some openings left by healed piercing are so large the holes do not successfully close once the object keeping them open is removed. That good-sized hole in your tongue or lip may be something you have to live with for life, with or without the ring or bar in place. Grafting to close the hole may be an option. In addition to the cost, however, the grafting procedure may result in visible scarring.

Appendix A

Problems with Practitioners – Whom to Call

Dentists, dental specialists, dental hygienists and denturists are members of controlled professions. They practise under strict legislative guidelines. In order to treat clients, each practitioner must be registered with or licensed by the appropriate provincial or state regulatory body. This agency oversees the quality of professional conduct of its members under the mandate of protection of the public.

Under legislative guidelines, regulatory agencies must periodically review the competence of their members. They are also required to investigate and provide remediation when a dental client files a complaint regarding the actions of a practitioner during client-practitioner professional interaction.

Therefore, clients experiencing difficulties that cannot be resolved through frank, non-aggressive discussion with their practitioners have resolutions at their disposal. Such difficulties include perception of harm caused by a practitioner, inappropriate sexual behaviour, unethical or illegal conduct. For remedies to these problems, the client should contact the regulatory agency that oversees the practice of the professional involved.

Each of the dental professions also has federal and provincial (state) associations that promote lifelong learning, ethics and professional responsibility among practitioners. Although membership in most of these professional associations is voluntary, competent, ethical practitioners are usually active members.

Dental professional organizations at the federal level have web sites to provide information to their members and to the general public. Some of these web addresses are provided at the end of this appendix. These sites also contain web addresses (if available) of their constituent provincial, territorial or state associations and regulatory bodies. If a particular constituent organization does not maintain a web site, other contact information is provided.

Addresses and telephone numbers for local, provincial, territorial or state professional associations may also be found using an on-line phone directory search if you know the full name of the appropriate agency.

Local dental study groups are often found in urban areas. Such an organization can also be a source of information about access to care and to the regulatory agencies that monitor the professions.

Web Sites for Federal Dental Professional Associations – North America

Dentistry

The Canadian Dental Association .... www.cda-adc.ca
To access information on provincial and territorial dental associations:
Click on "Provincial and Territorial Dental Associations" and then
        "Provincial Regulatory Authorities and Provincial Associations"

The American Dental Association .... www.ada.org
To access information on constituent (state) professional associations:
Click on "Dental Organizations" and then
        "Constituent (state) Associations"

Dental Hygiene

The Canadian Dental Hygienists Association .... www.cdha.ca
To access information on provincial and territorial dental hygiene associations:
Click on "Career" and then
        "Choose Your Province"

The American Dental Hygienists Association .... www.adha.org
To access information on the constituent (state) professional associations:
Click on "Related Links" and then
        "State Dental Hygiene Associations"

Denturists

Denturist Association of Canada .... www.denturist.org
To access information on provincial and territorial denturist associations and regulatory bodies:
Click on "Members and Affiliates" and then
        "Provincial and Territorial Associations" or
        "Provincial and Territorial Regulatory Bodies"

Appendix B

Client Cost Ranges for Dental Services

Not only will diligent oral self care prevent pain and suffering in a physical sense, it will reduce the pain in your wallet. This is especially true for individuals and families who do not have dental insurance.

Insurance providers have specific guidelines regarding treatment services covered and the dollar amounts reimbursable for each service. Many companies also restrict time frames in which payment for routine treatments such as examinations and dental cleanings can be claimed. Even with good insurance coverage most clients can expect to pay some percentage of the fees charged by the practitioner.

Insured clients with complex dental care needs who want treatment usually are required to have the dentist prepare a treatment plan and fee determination for submission to the insurer. The company will then advise the practitioner and the insured client what portion of the fee will be covered by the plan. This should be completed prior to provision of care and may take several weeks.

Most professional associations publish fee guides for their members. These documents detail the suggested fee ranges for a comprehensive list of oral treatment services. Many practitioners follow these guides closely.

However, each practitioner is legally allowed to charge a fee s/he determines is appropriate for treatment rendered. A practitioner may charge a fee below or above the range in their established fee guide. While most clients will not question a lower fee, those who feel they are being charged excessively have a legitimate cause for notifying the practitioner's regulatory body for clarification, complaint or possible redress.

The following tables indicate current fee ranges you might pay a general practitioner in Canada for the most commonly performed dental treatments. Specialist fee ranges are usually higher. **All fees are listed in Canadian dollars and are based on the 2010 Ontario fee guide.**

Restorative Treatment: Fillings

Amalgam (silver-coloured)	Primary (baby) Tooth	Permanent Tooth
1 tooth surface restored	50-60	50-75
2 tooth surfaces restored	100-110	100-125
3 tooth surfaces restored	115-125	115-155
4 tooth surfaces restored	125-205	125-205
special retention used: ▶ bonding ▶ pins (depends on number used)	Add 25-35 to above	Add 25-35 to above Add 15-75 to above
Composite Resin (tooth-coloured)		
1 tooth surface restored	95-120	95-120
2 tooth surfaces restored	125-150	125-200
3 tooth surfaces restored	150-300	165-300
4 tooth surfaces restored	150-300	170-325
Fee range allows for differences in complexity of fillings for front and back teeth.		

Restorative Treatment: Endodontic (Root Canal) Therapy

Single Tooth Treatment	Primary (baby) Tooth	Permanent Tooth
Tooth with 1 canal	145-160	385-595
Tooth with 2 canals	205-230	485-690
Tooth with 3 canals	205-230	675-1100
Tooth with 4 or more canals		780-1200

Restorative Treatment: Crowns

Crowns (caps), 1 Tooth	Primary (baby) Tooth	Permanent Tooth
Metal ▶ pre-formed ▶ custom-fitted ▶ implant-supported	160-180	160-180 530-595 665-735
Pre-formed plastic	160-180	160-180
Metal with tooth-coloured veneer ▶ acrylic ▶ porcelain ▶ implant-supported		465-510 625-690 665-735
Porcelain ▶ implant-supported		625-690 665-735
Fees quoted do not include those charged by the dental lab for production of the restoration where applicable. These fees are charged back to the client.		

Oral Surgical Services*

* Assumes the client is in good health and treatment is provided using local anaesthesia only.

Single Tooth Removal	Permanent Tooth
Tooth visible (uncomplicated)	105-120
Tooth visible (complicated)	170-190
Tooth impacted (covered with soft tissue and possibly bone)	170-280
Tooth impacted (complicated)	340-410
Periodontal Surgery	
Soft tissue graft (per site)	470-520
Connective tissue graft (per site)	635-700
Bone grafts (per site)	890-1125

Pain Management

For medically compromised clients, hospital facilities may be required to provide treatment safely. Some of the treatment costs may be covered by provincial health insurance plans.

General Anaesthesia	
Charged per unit of time (where 1 unit = 15 min.)	
► range quoted from 2-8 time units	145-515
► each additional unit over 8	45-60
Deep Sedation	
Charged per unit of time (where 1 unit = 15 min.)	
► range quoted from 2-8 time units	145-515
► each additional unit over 8	45-60
Conscious Sedation	
Charged per unit of time (where 1 unit = 15 min.)	
► range quoted from 1-8 time units	45-225
► each additional unit over 8	20-30

Restorative Treatment: Removable Dentures

Partial Dentures (replacing some of the teeth in the arch)	Permanent Teeth
Acrylic mandibular (lower) arch	275-300
Acrylic maxillary (upper) arch	275-300
Both arches completed at the same time	355-395
Acrylic and metal mandibular arch	475-525
Acrylic and metal maxillary arch	475-525
Both arches completed at the same time	650-720
Fee ranges are for provision of services relating to design and placement of the denture. Fees for examination, consultation and mouth preparation are charged separately. In addition, laboratory fees for production of the appliance are charged back to the client. The client also will be charged for post-denture-placement adjustments and relines.	
Complete Dentures (replacing all the teeth in the arch)	
Mandibular (lower) arch	650-720
Maxillary (upper) arch	650-720
Both arches completed at the same time	1070-1180

Orthodontic Treatment

Fees for preliminary examinations, diagnostic records and pre-treatment consultation appointments are charged separately from costs of the treatment.

Due to the range of complexity of cases requiring orthodontic intervention, only the simplest procedures are included in the table.

Appliance Therapy	Permanent Teeth
Space maintainers:	
▶ cast metal crown with attachment	230-275
▶ band and wire loop (1 side of the arch)	115-125
▶ lingual arch (whole arch)	230-255
▶ acrylic removable	145-160
▶ acrylic removable with teeth	170-190
▶ acrylic removable space regaining	195-215
▶ acrylic removable crossbite correction	195-215
Fixed appliances ▶ 1 arch ▶ both arches	Fees assessed on an individual case basis.
Post-treatment retainers (per arch)	
▶ removable	150-165
▶ fixed	180-200
Does not include dental lab fees to produce the appliance. Lab fees are charged back to the client.	

Dental Disease Prevention Services

Client Examination	Primary (baby) Teeth	Permanent Teeth
Initial visit with diagnosis and consultation	55-95	115-125
Radiographs (x-rays): ▶ single intra-oral view ▶ full-mouth series ▶ two bitewing views ▶ four bitewing views ▶ panoramic view (full dentition) ▶ cephalogram (one) ▶ cephalogram (two)	20-25 100-115 25-30	20-25 110-120 25-30 35-40 50-60 45-55 65-75
Recall/recare visual exam	20-30	20-30
Exam and evaluation for a specific condition or emergency visit	25-125	25-125
Teeth Cleaning Services*		
Scaling and root planing	45-55 per time unit	
Tooth polishing	30-40 per time unit	
Disease Prevention Services*		
One-to-one personal oral self-care instruction	35-45 per time unit	
Application of desensitizing agents	45-55 per unit of time	
Fluoride application: ▶ rinse (supervised self-administered) ▶ professional application	15-20 20-25	
*Fees are based on units of time required to complete the procedure (where 1 unit = 15 min.)		

Cosmetic Services

Tooth-whitening Services	Permanent Teeth
In-office bleaching (vital teeth) ▶ 1-3 time units ▶ Each additional unit over 3	55-185 55-60
In-office bleaching of non-vital tooth/teeth ▶ 1-3 time units ▶ Each additional unit over 3	30-105 30-35
Customized tray and home bleaching materials	Fees assessed on an individual basis.
Fees are based on units of time required to complete the procedure (where 1 unit = 15 min.)	
Tooth-coloured Veneer Application	
Per tooth – acrylic	215-330
Per tooth – porcelain	420-460
Does not include dental lab fee where applicable. Lab fees are charged back to the client.	

Miscellaneous

Custom Mouthguard (Sports Type)	Permanent Teeth
Does not include dental lab fees to produce the appliance. Lab fees are charged back to the client.	100-120
Nightguard or Bite Plane	
To prevent teeth-grinding habit	230-255
To treat jaw joint pain	235-270
Does not include dental lab fees to produce the appliance. Lab fees are charged back to the client.	
Appliance adjustments per unit of time (where 1 unit = 15 min.)	55-65

Glossary

Acute: a term used to describe disease events that are significant and of short duration.

Alveolar bone: the spongy bone that surrounds tooth roots and supports the teeth in the mouth.

Alveolitis: an infection of alveolar bone following tooth removal.

Amalgam: a silver-coloured dental filling material made up of a combination of metals mixed with mercury.

Anaesthetic (general): a substance used to induce a state of unconsciousness where the individual's protective reflexes (gagging, swallowing, etc.) are absent.

Anaesthetic (local): a substance used to induce the absence of sensation to a particular area of the body.

Analgesic: medication designed to reduce pain.

Antibiotics: drugs that destroy certain strains of bacteria. They are not effective against viruses.

Antimicrobial agents: substances that destroy or control the growth of micro-organisms.

Antiseptics: substances that reduce the number and control the growth of disease-producing micro-organisms.

Arch wire: a specially designed wire that fits into brackets attached to teeth so that the teeth move to desired locations.

Attached gingiva: the soft tissue that covers the alveolar bone supporting the teeth in the mouth.

Baby teeth: see deciduous teeth or primary teeth.

Bacterial plaque: organized colonies of species of bacteria found in the mouth. These colonies stick to teeth in areas that are hard to clean mechanically.

Behaviour modeling: a process during which a comfortable client undergoes dental treatment while being observed by a client who is fearful of that same treatment.

Bicuspid (premolar): a type of tooth that has at least two elevations (cusps) on its biting surface.

Biological film (biofilm): name used to describe organized colonies of oral bacteria that stick to tooth surfaces in areas of the mouth that are difficult to clean mechanically.

Bottle mouth decay: see infant caries syndrome.

Bridge: see fixed bridge.

Calculus: hard oral deposits on teeth caused by the buildup and mineralization of bacterial plaque or biofilm.

Canine (cuspid): a type of tooth with one sharp, pointed biting edge.

Cap: see crown.

Caries: tooth decay.

Cast: a plaster or stone model of a tooth or the mouth used in a dental lab to make restorations or oral appliances.

Cavity preparation: the removal of diseased tooth tissue in order to place filling material to return the tooth to its normal shape and function.

Cementum: the mineralized tissue covering the root of a tooth.

Cephalogram: an x-ray of the head that shows the teeth in relationship with the bones of the face. It is used to diagnose malocclusions and determine appropriate treatment plans.

Cervical line: the junction of the enamel tissue covering the crown and the cementum tissue covering the root of a tooth.

Cervix: the narrowed area between the crown and the root of a tooth.

Chromogenic: literally "colour-producing"; term used to describe micro-organisms that can stain tooth surfaces.

Chronic: a term used to describe diseases that persist over a long period of time.

Composite resin: a plastic filling material that can be shaded to match tooth enamel.

Congenital: existing or present at birth.

Coping: the metal attachment to a bone-implant device which protrudes through the gum tissue and interfaces with the oral appliance (denture).

Crossbites: any deviation from normal horizontal overlap of the upper teeth when they bite against the lower teeth.

Crown: a restoration that replaces the whole crown portion of a tooth.

Cusp: a pointed elevation on the biting surface of a tooth.

Cuspid (canine): a type of tooth with one sharp, pointed biting edge.

Cystic fibrosis: an inherited condition in which normal enzymes that support digestive and lung function are absent.

Deciduous (primary) teeth: the first set of human teeth. Some of these teeth are in function between six months and 12 years of age as they emerge and are gradually replaced by permanent teeth.

Demineralization: the removal of minerals from the hard tissues of the teeth by acids present in the mouth.

Dental bridge: a fixed appliance that replaces a missing tooth (or adjacent teeth in the same arch).

Dental floss: specialized thread used to disturb oral biofilm from hard-to-reach areas between teeth.

Dental implant: a metal device that is surgically placed in oral tissue to support a replacement for a single tooth or to support a denture.

Dental impressions: prints of the teeth and oral structures made by placing a tray containing soft material over the tissues. When the material sets, the tray is removed.

Dentin: the tissue that makes up the greatest percentage of tooth bulk. It lies under the enamel and cementum.

Denture (complete): a removable appliance constructed to replace teeth in one dental arch when they have all been lost.

Denture (partial): a removable appliance constructed to replace multiple teeth missing in one dental arch.

Denturist: a registered dental practitioner whose scope of practice includes making and fitting of dentures.

Desensitizing agents: compounds applied to exposed root surfaces to reduce tooth sensitivity to temperature changes and acidic foods.

Deviant swallow: a pattern of swallowing in which the tongue is thrust forward between the front teeth instead of curling up and backwards along the palate.

Emphysema: a chronic lung condition that interferes with breathing and oxygen exchange in the lungs.

Enamel: the hard mineralized outer tissue of tooth crowns.

Enamel sealant: a thin layer of plastic material bonded to grooved biting surfaces of newly emerged premolar and molar teeth to reduce the risk of decay.

Endodontics (root canal therapy): the procedures to remove diseased pulp tissue from the inside of infected teeth.

Endodontist: a dental practitioner who specializes in root canal therapy.

Eruption: the process by which teeth move into the mouth from below the soft tissue.

Exfoliation: the process by which primary (baby) teeth naturally become loose and are shed.

Extrinsic: pertaining to the tooth surface, e.g. extrinsic stain that is on the surface and can be removed.

Fear hierarchy: part of the psychological treatment process of systematic desensitization. The fearful individual lists the aspects of an event in order from least upsetting to most feared.

Fixed bridge: a permanent restoration used to replace a single or small number of adjacent teeth in the same arch when healthy teeth are available on both ends of the space. Crowns are fitted on the teeth bordering the space and a biting surface is created to fill the gap.

Floss holder: a handle to hold dental floss to be used to clean between teeth.

Floss threader: a small device used to carry dental floss under fixed bridges or orthodontic arch wires.

Free gingiva: the soft gum tissue that lies against the neck of a tooth like a turtleneck sweater.

Gingiva (gums): the soft tissue that covers the alveolar bone and lies snuggly against the necks of teeth.

Gingival sulcus: the v-shaped trough between the crown of the tooth and the soft tissue (gingiva) that lies against the neck of the tooth but is not attached to it.

Gingivectomy: a periodontal treatment procedure involving the removal or repositioning of the free gingiva to create a gingival sulcus of appropriate depth.

Gingivitis: a reversible inflammation of the soft tissues of the mouth caused by oral bacteria.

Gingivoplasty: a periodontal treatment procedure that involves surgical correction of the location of free gingival tissue and establishment of an appropriate gingival sulcus depth.

Graft: the transfer of tissue from one part of the mouth to another.

Gums: see gingiva.

Halitosis: persistent abnormal mouth odour; causes include the presence of oral, respiratory or gastric disease.

HARP (Healing Arts Radiation Protection Act): legislation in Ontario, Canada, which defines and controls the use of diagnostic and therapeutic radiation.

Head gear: an appliance used in orthodontic treatment which has components that fit into the mouth and parts that are outside the mouth. It is used to hold back jaw growth, move posterior teeth backward in the mouth or provide anchorage when front teeth are moved backward in the arch.

Host resistance: the natural defenses of the body against disease.

Implant: a metal device surgically placed to support a replacement for a single missing tooth or for a partial or complete denture.

Incisor: a type of tooth that has a single sharp linear biting edge; located at the front of the mouth.

Infant caries syndrome: severe tooth decay in young children that affects most of the primary teeth at an early age.

Inherited: used to describe individual characteristics or conditions that are passed from one generation to the next through the genes.

Interproximal: the term used to describe the spaces between adjacent teeth in the same arch.

Interproximal brush: a small cylindrical or wedge-shaped toothbrush useful for cleaning the sides of adjacent teeth in the same arch below their points of contact.

Intrinsic: pertaining to something that is part of the tooth structure.

Leeway space: extra space in the dental arches available when primary cuspids and molars are replaced by permanent cuspids and premolars.

Ligature: a wire or elastic used to tie orthodontic arch wires into brackets attached to each individual tooth.

Local: describing a condition that is restricted to a small part of the mouth.

Malocclusion: when the teeth in the upper and lower arches meet (bite) in an abnormal relationship.

Maryland bridge: a fixed restoration to replace a single tooth (usually at the front of the mouth) that is bonded to the tooth (or teeth) adjacent to the space.

Model: see cast.

Molar: any of the large teeth at the back of the mouth used for grinding food.

Normal bacterial flora: micro-organisms which live in and on body surfaces at all times without causing disease.

Occlusion: the relationship between the teeth in the upper and lower arches when the mouth is closed in biting position.

Openbite: occurs where there is no overlap of upper teeth with lower ones when the mouth is closed in biting position.

Oral irrigation: the use of antimicrobial fluids to control bacterial growth by directing them into the gingival sulcus. Use of an oral irrigation device may also be helpful for removing food debris during orthodontic treatment.

Oral mucosa: the soft tissue lining the cheeks and lips.

Orthodontics: the specialty dental practice of straightening teeth.

Orthodontist: the dental specialist who diagnoses and treats malocclusions (crooked teeth).

Overbite: the amount of vertical overlap of the upper front teeth (central incisors) with the lower front teeth (central incisors) when the mouth is closed and the biting surfaces of the back teeth are in contact.

Overdenture: an appliance used to replace most of the natural teeth missing in one arch. The few remaining teeth with healthy root structures can be prepared and the denture made to fit over these teeth to provide better retention and chewing function.

Overjet (horizontal overbite): the distance between the tongue side of the upper front teeth (central incisors) and the lip-facing surface of the lower central incisors measured in a horizontal plane when the mouth is closed and the biting surfaces of the back teeth are in contact.

Panoramic radiograph: an x-ray taken of the lower face using a film that is held outside the mouth.

Pathogenic: term used to describe micro-organisms which cause disease.

Periodontal ligament: a band of connective tissue fibres that attach at one end to the alveolar bone of the tooth socket and at the other to the cementum tissue covering the tooth root.

Periodontal pocket: any area of gingival sulcus around the tooth that is deeper than three millimetres.

Periodontics: the dental specialty dealing with diseases of the supporting tissues of the teeth and soft tissues of the mouth.

Periodontist: the dental specialist who deals with diseases of oral soft tissues and those that support teeth.

Periodontitis: an irreversible disease that destroys soft tissue and alveolar bone that supports teeth.

Permanent (secondary) teeth: the second set of teeth which humans develop and are meant to last a lifetime.

Phobia: extreme fear of an object or situation which results in avoidance.

Plaque: see biological film.

Premolar: a type of tooth in the permanent dentition that has two or more points on the biting surface.

Primary (baby) teeth: the first set of teeth that humans develop. The teeth erupt and function between approximately six months and 12 years of age and are all replaced by permanent teeth.

Proximal: the term used to describe the surfaces of adjacent teeth in the same arch that face each other.

Radiograph: a processed x-ray picture of a part of the body.

Root canal therapy: see endodontics.

Root planing: the use of instruments to smooth root surfaces of teeth.

Resorption: the natural process by which specialized cells remove the roots of primary teeth so they then fall out.

Restoration: the name applied to the replacement of the diseased (decayed) portion of a tooth to restore its shape and function; may be made of various materials, e.g. amalgam, composite resin, gold.

Rubber dam: a sheet of flexible latex or vinyl with holes through which teeth protrude. It is used to keep the operative area dry and to prevent debris created during the restorative process from being swallowed or inhaled.

Scaling: removal of hard deposits from teeth above and below the gum line.

Soft toothpicks: toothpicks made of pliable materials, useful in removing food debris and plaque from between teeth.

Sulcus brush: a small toothbrush with a single tuft of bristles on each end of the handle, designed to disturb biofilm along the gum line.

Systematic desensitization: a treatment process designed to help people overcome phobias to specific events. Components include a combination of physical relaxation techniques, imagining the feared situation and positive thinking.

Systemic: a word used to describe a condition that affects many or all parts of the body, usually caused when agents (micro-organisms, drugs, etc.) access the bloodstream.

Tartar: see calculus.

Tongue thrust: see deviant swallow.

Tooth evulsion: loss of an intact whole tooth, usually as a result of a traumatic injury to the face.

Tooth intrusion: forcing of a tooth into its bony socket as a result of a traumatic injury; most commonly seen with baby teeth or partly erupted permanent front teeth.

Veneer: thin layer of restorative material applied to the surface of a tooth to change its shape, size or colour.

Veneer crown: a restoration used to replace the entire crown portion of a diseased tooth. It is made of metal for strength, covered with a thin layer of tooth-coloured material for aesthetics.

Virulence: a term used to describe the potential of micro-organisms to cause disease.

Wedge-shaped toothpicks: made of soft wood, they are useful to remove food debris and disturb plaque between teeth without damaging soft tissue.

References

American Heart Association: *Antibiotic Prophylaxis Recommendations Prior to Dental Treatment.* (2007)

American Academy of Orthopedic Surgeons: *Antibiotic Prophylaxis Recommendations Prior to Dental Treatment.* (2007)

Andrews, Esther K. *Practice Management for Dental Hygienists.* Lippincott Williams & Wilkins. Philadelphia, New York, London. (2007)

Beemsterboer, Phyllis L. *Ethics and Law in Dental Hygiene.* W.B. Saunders Company. Philadelphia, New York, Toronto. (2001)

Bird, Doni L. and Robinson, Debbie S. Torres and Ehrlich *Modern Dental Assisting,* 9th ed. Saunders Elsevier. St. Louis, Missouri. (2009)

Brand, Richard W. and Isselhard, Donald E. *Anatomy of Orofacial Structures,* 7th ed. Mosby. St. Louis, Missouri. (2003)

Burt, Brian A. and Eklund, Stephen A. *Dentistry, Dental Practice and the Community,* 6th ed. Elsevier Saunders. St. Louis, Missouri. (2005)

Darby, Michele Leonardi and Walsh, Margaret S. *Dental Hygiene Theory and Practice.* 2nd ed. Saunders. St. Louis, Missouri. (2003)

Hatrick, Carol Dixon, Eakle, W. Stephen and Bird, William F. *Dental Materials: Clinical Application for Dental Assistants and Dental Hygienists.* Saunders. St. Louis, Missouri. (2003)

Haveles, Elena Bablenis. *Applied Pharmacology for the Dental Hygienist.* 5th ed. Mosby. St. Louis, Missouri. (2007)

Ibsen, Olga A.C. and Phelan, Joan Andersen. *Oral Pathology for the Dental Hygienist.* 4th ed. Saunders. St. Louis, Missouri. (2004)

Kimbrough, Vickie J. and Lautar, Charla J. Ethics, *Jurisprudence and Practice Management in Dental Hygiene.* 2nd ed. Prentice Hall. Upper Saddle River, New Jersey. (2006)

Melfi, Rudy C. and Alley, Keith E. *Permar's Oral Embryology and Microscopic Anatomy.* 10th ed. Lippincott Williams & Wilkins. (2000)

Miller, Chris H. and Palenik, Charles John. *Infection Control and Management of Hazardous Materials for the Dental Team.* 3rd ed. Elsevier Mosby. St. Louis, Missouri. (2005)

Palmer, Carole A. *Diet and Nutrition in Oral Health.* 2nd ed. Pearson Prentice Hall. Upper Saddle River, New Jersey. (2007)

Pickett, Frieda Atherton and Terézhalmy, Géza T. *Dental Drug Reference with Clinical Applications.* Lippincott Williams & Wilkins. Baltimore and Philadelphia. (2006)

Tortora, Gerard J. and Derrickson, Bryan. *Introduction to the Human Body: the essentials of anatomy and physiology.* 7th ed. John Wiley and Sons. New York. (2007)

Weinberg, Mea A., Westphal, Cheryl and Froum, Stuart J. *Comprehensive Periodontics for the Dental Hygienist.* 2nd ed. Pearson, Prentice Hall. Upper Saddle River, New Jersey. (2006)

Wilkins, Esther M. *Clinical Practice of the Dental Hygienist.* 9th ed. Lippincott Williams & Wilkins. (2005)

Wood, Samuel E., Wood, Eileen, Wood, Ellen R. *The World of Psychology.* 3rd Canadian ed. Pearson, Allyn & Bacon. Toronto. (2003)

Index